"Oftentimes, standing between us and our destiny are lies from the enemy about who ⟨...⟩ what we're eligible ⟨...⟩ of. *Redefined* will help you ⟨...⟩ them with the truth of who y⟨...⟩ step fully into all he has des⟨...⟩

C⟨...⟩ ⟨...⟩ bestselling ⟨...⟩ ;
founder, A21 and Propel Women

"I highly recommend reading Arden Bevere's book *Redefined: Confronting the Labels That Limit Us*. God doesn't label us; he calls us. This book will help you completely redefine what you have been called to do and who you are called to be."

Jentezen Franklin, senior pastor, Free Chapel;
New York Times bestselling author

"In every generation God calls new leaders to share his love, power, and truth to those around them. Arden Bevere has answered that call, and in *Redefined: Confronting the Labels That Limit Us,* he extends it to millennials and anyone longing to make a positive difference in our world. Using contemporary examples and the timeless truth of God's Word, *Redefined* strips away false assumptions and mistaken generalizations and reminds us of our true identities as God's sons and daughters."

Chris Hodges, senior pastor, Church of the Highlands;
author of *The Daniel Dilemma* and *What's Next?*

"Arden, you have stood up and taken notice of the cry of this generation. You are giving them the keys to overcome the labels that have been placed on them to keep them small and keep them from changing their world. We truly believe that this book is a necessary tool that needs to be placed in the hands of every young person who is struggling to know why they are here and what they are meant to do. When we know our identity in Christ, the labels that are given to us have no power. Thank you for taking the time to write these words. I know that because of you, this generation can and will change the world for the better as they respond to their calling in Christ."

Pastor Henry and Alex Seeley, cofounders
of The Belonging Co.

"When Arden asked me to read the first chapter of *Redefined*, my expectation was to hear the words of a millennial who loves God. However, I was overwhelmed with amazement by what I read. I heard a young man, who is very much in touch with the challenges of his generation but speaks to them with the wisdom of a fifty-year-old. I was inspired, encouraged, and challenged, and my faith was built to new levels. I was in awe, for I received life-transforming revelation knowledge that could only be given by the Holy Spirit.

Arden is a leader, who loves God deeply, passionately loves his family, and is tender and compassionate to all he comes in contact with. The fruit of the Spirit that stands out in his life is faithfulness.

I feel privileged to be his father, but I know he is a gift to the body of Christ at large. I know your life will be changed not only by the words of his message but also by the strength of this young man's heart."

John Bevere, bestselling author and minister;
cofounder of Messenger International

"Arden has labored tirelessly over this message for years. *Redefined* is more than a book; it is a clarion call to a generation who knows they are destined for something *more* and won't be constrained by labels that suggest something *less*. Each chapter debunks another word that has sought to systematically undermine all that God has woven within his sons and daughters."

Lisa Bevere, bestselling author and minister;
cofounder of Messenger International

"Arden Bevere brings a new and fresh perspective to an ancient yet still applicable truth. The world attempts to label us by our actions but God calls us according to his plans. This message is for everyone who has allowed the wrong labels to keep them from fulfilling their destiny. I believe this book has the power to change your life."

Justin Dailey, lead pastor, Action Church

REDEFINED

CONFRONTING THE LABELS THAT LIMIT US

ARDEN BEVERE

Revell

a division of Baker Publishing Group
Grand Rapids, Michigan

© 2021 by Arden Bevere

Published by Revell
a division of Baker Publishing Group
PO Box 6287, Grand Rapids, MI 49516-6287
www.revellbooks.com

Printed in the United States of America

Library of Congress Cataloging-in-Publication Data
Names: Bevere, Arden, 1994– author.
Title: Redefined : confronting the labels that limit us / Arden Bevere.
Description: Grand Rapids, Michigan : Revell, a division of Baker Publishing
    Group, [2021]
Identifiers: LCCN 2020036042 I ISBN 9780800737573 (paperback) I ISBN
    9780800740399 (casebound)
Subjects: LCSH: Identity (Psychology)—Religious aspects—Christianity.
Classification: LCC BV4509.5 .B485 2021 I DDC 248.4—dc23
LC record available at https://lccn.loc.gov/2020036042

Some names and details have been changed to protect the privacy of the individuals involved.

The author is represented by The Fedd Agency.

21 22 23 24 25 26 27   7 6 5 4 3 2 1

CONTENTS

ONE

THE **POWER** OF A **WORD**

Handle them carefully, for words have more power than atom bombs.

Pearl Strachan Hurd

FROM THE MOMENT we are born, the words spoken over us begin to mold our identity, for better or for worse. Relatives, teachers, and peers comment on our appearance, our character, and our personality. As we grow, these words begin to accumulate in our mind and build an image of who we are, or more accurately, who we *think* we are or should be.

The reality that words have the power to identify and shape us first struck me while I was researching a project at work. I'd been asked to come up with some ways the ministry I was working with could more effectively reach people in my generation. As I brainstormed, I began to realize that the first step to reach and serve my peers was to gain a better understanding of how they see themselves. So

I posted this question on my Facebook page: If you could describe the young adult generation today in one word, what would it be?

The answers that came in were almost as surprising as the speed with which they were posted: *Lost. Unhappy. Searching. Hungry. Distracted. Lazy. Broken. Lacking. Entitled. Disillusioned.* There were some positive words sprinkled in as well, but the majority of the responses were negative.

It broke my heart to see the way people view my generation. I was especially saddened to see that many of the responses were from my peers: people in their twenties and thirties. These words expressed what they believed to be true about themselves. My people, my generation, described themselves as so much less than they are called to be.

As I read through the comments, God began to place some passages from the Bible in my heart that declare the opposite of the negative words people had written. One verse that especially stood out to me was 1 Peter 2:9.

> But you are not like that, for you are a chosen people. You are royal priests, a holy nation, God's very own possession. As a result, you can show others the goodness of God, for he called you out of the darkness into his wonderful light. (NLT)

It would be an understatement to say that God's view of us is positive. This description is bursting with pride and excitement. The passage uses words like *chosen, royal,* and *holy.* We belong to him. We are called with a holy purpose.

Just as importantly, note what this verse does not say—that we are lost, lazy, entitled, or broken. In other words, we are not doomed or obligated to live up to the negative labels that we have placed on ourselves—quite the opposite! We are called to fulfill God's plans and live up to his expectations.

Here's the problem for twenty- and thirtysomethings though. At our age and stage of life, things get real. Scary real. And in the face of uncertainty and adversity, if we don't truly know who we are, we will fall back on the words spoken over us and the image of ourselves that we've built from them. We will choose careers, navigate relationships, and build families under the shadow of critical self-labels and a negative self-image.

Rather than living under those negative shadows, however, we must realize something: a label limits us to how the world sees us. A label speaks to who we are now, and it limits us to what has already happened. That is the tendency of the world and society around us—to define ourselves based on our past or present.

A calling, on the other hand, speaks to the future, to whom God has created us to be and what he plans for us to do. Our calling is based on God's original design for us. It goes beyond the trauma or pain we have been through, the mistakes we have committed, and the circumstances we are in right now.

Our calling trumps labels every time. Labels shrink our world; callings enlarge our world. Labels disqualify and limit us; callings qualify and release us. Labels are temporary; callings are eternal.

CALL TO A GENERATION

Our generation is called to change the world. I truly believe that. But in order to step into our full potential and true identity, we must *redefine* the way we see ourselves. We must listen to the right voices and believe the right words. We must confront and reject the labels that limit us and restore the calling of God that defines us.

Before you can confront something, though, you have to identify it. That's why the apostle Paul wrote, "I do not fight like a boxer beating the air" (1 Cor. 9:26). Paul knew his goal in life, and he knew what he was fighting.

In this book, I will unpack ten negative words that are often spoken about our generation—both by others and by us—and I will compare and contrast them to what God's Word says about us. For each negative term, there is a corresponding positive term that focuses on the identity and calling God has given us.

These are not the expected, obvious opposites though. They are more like companion words: concepts that reveal the positive truths hidden by negative labels. The more I studied the labels people use to describe our generation, the more I realized they actually point to deeper issues of self-worth, of character, and of value. The positive terms I have chosen to focus on are specifically designed to counteract these underlying problems.

That's what the title of this book means. It's about a change of perspective, a change of definition, and a change of value. We can't and we shouldn't try to change the essence of our generation. We are who we are. We are valued and loved by God. We are called for such a time as this. But we *can* and *must* allow God to show us how he sees us. We must let his perspective redefine ours.

And while my main goal is to help us realize that we have more options than just the lost and entitled generation, the biblical truths condensed in each chapter are applicable to all generations and can challenge and lead anyone, regardless of their age.

Before we break down these words, let's consider the magnitude of the human language and how quickly our vocabulary increases as we grow older. According to a blog called *Word Counter*, the average one-year-old will recognize roughly fifty words. This increases to five thousand words by age four and then to ten thousand by age eight.[1]

My oldest brother, Addison, is one of those people who has an incredibly expansive vocabulary. When we talk, he often uses terms I don't understand. If I ask him what in the world he's talking about, he'll give me the simple word, the word "normal" people use, to explain what he means. My response is always the same: "Why didn't you just say that?"

My point is that with over one million words in the English language, we have a plethora of terms at our disposal. We don't have to settle for the words that are always used, and we must be intentional about choosing new ones. The Bible says the words we speak can bring either life or death (Prov. 18:21). For every negative word of death, there are thousands of words of life that could be used in its place. We have the power to reimagine the words spoken over us and thereby redirect the trajectory of our lives.

I was heartbroken when reading the answers to my Facebook question because I know this generation is called to be world changers, but so many of us have failed to realize that potential. We have been speaking the wrong words over ourselves because we haven't allowed our creator to define us. We were designed by God to make a difference here on earth, but in order to do that, we must reject false labels and choose to agree with the way God sees us.

COHEIRS WITH CHRIST

When we know who we are, we know how we should live. My parents helped me learn this early in life. They used to tell my brothers and me that we were princes. *Princes?* Most little girls like to be called princesses, but as little boys, we were not so enthusiastic at our parents' labeling. To add to our confusion, they didn't call us princes when we were acting right but when we were acting *out* instead. After we had done something we shouldn't have, they would look us right in the eyes and say, "You are a prince, and princes do not act like that." They didn't call us princes because of our family ancestry or because we resembled the heroes of the latest Disney movie. No, they were referring to our place as children of God. They helped us see that we are called to a higher standard, because God adopted us as coheirs with Christ (Rom. 8:17).

At the time, of course, I didn't fully understand the significance behind their lesson. But as I grew older, I learned to hold myself to the standards of a prince, a coheir of Christ. That doesn't mean I was perfect—far from it. I have made my share of mistakes, and I'm sure I'll make more. But as I look back over my teenage and early adult years, I know that I have always strived to align my decisions with that identity. I have made far more good choices than bad ones, and even when I have made poor choices, I've known deep inside it wasn't who I was. And that knowledge spurred me to adjust my lifestyle.

My point is not that I am better than anyone or that I have some superhuman level of self-control. Not even close. Rather, the identity my parents built into me by calling me a "prince" became an inner voice that shaped my self-image and directed many of my decisions. I am grateful to my parents for affirming my God-given identity in those formative years rather than labeling me based on my negative behavior or mistakes.

FIGHTING WITH OUR IDENTITIES INTACT

My mom often told her boys that the spiritual attacks we go through in life are more based on who we are going to become rather than who we currently are or who we used to be. In other words, the enemy will try to get us to question our identity so he can stop us from fulfilling our God-given calling. He wants us to doubt who we are called to be. If he can destroy our purpose, then he can more easily influence our behavior.

Remember how 1 Peter 2:9 describes us: a chosen people, a royal priesthood, a holy nation, God's special possession who declares his praises. With that kind of calling and that big of a future, it's no wonder the enemy tries to attack our sense of identity every chance he gets. The enemy would not attack someone unless he is threatened by them. Who would he be threatened by? Citizens of heaven. World changers. Sons and daughters of God.

We see an example of this when Satan tested Jesus after he spent forty days fasting and praying in the wilderness. Jesus had just started his ministry, and the devil came to tempt him.

The tempter came to him and said, "If you are the Son of God, tell these stones to become bread." (Matt. 4:3)

The enemy's first strategy was to challenge Jesus's *identity* in order to provoke wrong *actions*. He hoped insecurity would lead Jesus to make wrong choices. In this case, he wanted to lead Jesus into an empty, selfish display of power and into satisfying his own human needs outside of God's plan. He was trying to cause Jesus to sin, so he attacked his sense of identity.

Remember, the devil knew who Jesus was. He didn't doubt that Jesus was the Son of God. Rather, he was trying to use the rhetorical statement "if you are the Son of God" as a manipulative tactic to push Jesus into making a mistake.

But Jesus didn't flinch. He didn't back down. Rather than reacting out of insecurity, he responded with confidence. He knew that doing what the enemy wanted wouldn't prove his identity, and he knew he didn't have anything to prove in the first place. He was secure in his identity and mission. The devil's attack failed because there were no cracks of insecurity where his arrows of doubt could take effect.

The enemy will use the same strategy to attack you—not because he thinks you're weak, useless, or a nobody but because he knows your true identity and he is frightened by it. He will try to find insecurities and use them to move your focus off your true identity in Jesus and onto what he wants you to do in your own power. That probably won't be turning rocks into bread (even though that would be a neat party trick), but it will resemble similarly empty and self-focused attempts to prove your worth or create your own identity that is separate from God. If the enemy can distract you from who you are in Christ, then controlling your choices becomes far easier for him. As a child of God, you must have a firm understanding of who you are so that you can stay focused and avoid becoming deceived when tests and temptations come.

Jesus wasn't the only one who knew the importance of basing his identity in the Bible. In Acts 22, we find the apostle Paul facing off with a Roman officer. Paul was about to be flogged, which was one of the most painful punishments a person could endure. Victims were tied up, stretched out, and struck with a multitailed whip.

Just before the punishment began, Paul looked at the Roman officer and asked, "Is it legal for you to flog a Roman citizen who hasn't even been found guilty?" (v. 25). Paul was being tried as a Jew, which meant the Roman officials were denying him the rights and authority belonging to him as a Roman.

The man who was in charge of whipping Paul told his boss about Paul's Roman identity. As soon as the commanding officer realized who Paul was, he became very afraid, because he had not given Paul the treatment his citizenship mandated. He immediately began treating Paul differently.

If Paul had that much power just because he was a citizen of Rome, how much more power do we have as citizens of the kingdom of God? We, too, need to realize that, regardless of the challenges we face, we can stand on the rights and authority that come from our identity.

When the officers questioned Paul about his ancestry, he responded, "I was born a citizen" (v. 28). In the same way, each of us is born into the kingdom of God by faith. Whether you come from a Christian background or not, the moment you put your faith in Jesus, you were "born again" (John 3:3). You were given a new identity and a new purpose. You were called out of darkness and into freedom and victory!

Just like Jesus and Paul experienced, we can expect resistance, temptations, and attacks from the enemy. So how do we respond? First of all, we must *decide to fight*. When a soldier knows he is about to be attacked, he has two options: retreat or fight. In the same way, the knowledge that the enemy will attack our identity and sense of purpose can produce fear and paralysis, or it can motivate us to take a stand and fight back. It's our choice. We must decide not to give in to the assault against our generation but fight to be the people God has called us to be.

Our second response, once we have decided to fight, should be to *learn to fight well*. As soldiers in God's army, we are called to fight in faith through the power of the Word of God.

Jesus fought Satan's temptations in the wilderness by quoting Scripture, and Paul said the Word of God is like a sword (Eph. 6:17). Both Jesus and Paul knew that the Word of God is the most powerful weapon we can use against the devil.

> For the word of God is alive and active. Sharper than any double-edged sword, it penetrates even to dividing soul and spirit, joints and marrow; it judges the thoughts and attitudes of the heart. (Heb. 4:12)

Notice how God's Word has the power to peer deep into our own souls and hearts. It strengthens us, it teaches us truth, and it prepares us to stand against the lies of the enemy.

Like any weapon, we have to learn how to wield this sword. We must have it ingrained in our hearts so that our minds are not easily swayed from the truth. The more we know about what the Bible says regarding our identity, the less we will be affected by the attacks, temptations, and lies of the enemy.

My prayer is that this book would not just show you what the Bible says but that it would also prepare you for battle by teaching you how to speak the Word of God over your life and over our whole generation.

COMMUNITY LANGUAGE

Words are powerful in the life of an individual, but they are even more powerful when they are the common language of a community.

We see this power illustrated in the biblical story of the tower of Babel, which is found in Genesis and takes place after the worldwide flood described in Genesis 6. The writer of Genesis indicates that at this point in history, everyone in the region spoke the same language. They were unified in language and purpose—but their purpose was not the right one. They were actually disobeying God.

After the flood, God instructed Noah and his sons to spread out and fill the earth as their families grew and increased in number. But just a couple chapters later, we see the people had a different goal in mind.

> Come, let us build ourselves a city, with a tower that reaches to the heavens, so that we may make a name for ourselves. (Gen. 11:4)

Rather than spreading out to fill the earth, they banded together to build a city and a name for themselves, along with a tower that was probably a ziggurat, an ancient temple. In other words, they abandoned their relationship with God and united in rebellion against him. In response to their plans, God made a remarkable statement: "If as one people speaking the same language they have begun to do this, then nothing they plan to do will be impossible for them" (Gen. 11:6).

God knew that their plans would only lead them further away from him, so he caused them to speak different languages. This produced confusion, of course, and ultimately, they scattered to different parts of the earth, fulfilling God's original command.

Wow! This story highlights the power and potential within a group of people who speak the same language and rally around the same vision.

God didn't have a problem with his people speaking one language. His concern was that they were using their unity in disobedient and prideful ways. Imagine if their intentions had been good instead of destructive. Imagine if their vision centered around lifting up God's name instead of their own.

Now, imagine what *we* could do if we were united! That is my goal with this book—to bring our generation together under one language. I don't mean English or Spanish or French; I mean the same kingdom language. We must use our words for life not death and for building not destroying. We must be united in one righteous cause, not to make our name famous but to make God's name famous.

If the people of Babel were unified, God said, nothing would be impossible for them. I believe there is going to be a massive move of God's Spirit upon the earth, one that begins with youth and young adults and spreads to the entire world. But in order for us to bring about that change, we need to be united in heart and language under his Word. If we are, nothing we set out to do as sons and daughters of God will be impossible.

Do you see how powerful words can be? They determine our identity, they guide our actions, and they provide a common language to accomplish great things together. For the remainder of this book, we will look at the words often used to describe this generation and examine what they mean and represent, and then we'll replace them with words God uses to describe us. As we do, we're going to strengthen our foundations and grow into who God has called us to be.

Let's begin this journey together!

TWO

LOST

Not till we are lost, in other words not till we have lost
the world, do we begin to find ourselves.

Henry David Thoreau

BEING LOST is a scary thing. Imagine you're hiking through
Yosemite National Park. You walk down a familiar path, ad-
miring the tall sequoia trees, the lush undergrowth of the forest, and the occasional woodpecker or gray squirrel. The pull
of new vistas propels you onward, while your mind wanders
back to that first hiking trip you went on as a kid.

But as your mind meanders down memory lane, your feet
carry you into unknown territory. And before you know it,
you're lost. You don't see anything that resembles a path. You
wander around for a while, doing your best to retrace your
steps. But it's hard to recall because you were so wrapped
up in exploring your memories. You check your phone: no
service. Your heart rate increases. You walk around and

around, searching for anything that looks familiar, but nothing registers.

More bad news: you look up through the trees and notice that the sun is almost down. Nightfall is quickly approaching. You are forced to accept the fact that you're hopelessly lost. You can't find your way back, and you don't know where to go from here.

What would you be feeling? Desperation? Fear? Anxiety? Loneliness? Uncertainty?

We can probably all think of a time when we didn't know where we were going. Maybe, for you, a literal "lost in the woods" moment is vivid in your mind. Or maybe it's a time when you were lost, and Google Maps failed you miserably.

When we lose our direction, everything else becomes shaky and unstable.

Now transfer that feeling and that emotion to being lost in life. To a loss of direction when it comes to your existence. To a sense of confusion about where you're going as a human being. To a feeling of desperation, fear, and anxiety because you don't know what to do next. To pangs of loneliness because you have no one to turn to for help along the way.

It's a heavy feeling, isn't it? But it's necessary for our generation to talk about this because we have become lost in so many ways.

We've become lost in our purpose,
lost in our student loans,
lost in our relationships,
lost in our self-worth,
lost in our priorities,
lost in our phones.

It's no surprise, then, that we've become lost in our relationship with God too.

We are the generation with the greatest amount of *information*, but I fear we are also the generation with the least amount of spiritual *transformation*. Numerous surveys point out the tendency of millennials to abandon religion and traditional forms of faith. We have access to dozens of Bible translations, millions of Christian books, and an infinite number of God-centered teachings and podcasts and blogs. But even with all of this at our disposal, many people seem to be drifting further and further away from God.

Here's my point. We don't have to stay lost. We don't have to stumble through the lonely forest as night falls, wondering what to do or where to go. Whether we are talking about our life purpose, our relationships, or our spirituality, we must replace the term *lost* with a new term: *focused*.

FROM LOST TO FOCUSED

Focus refers to what we fix our eyes on. When we are lost, we don't know where to turn, which route to pursue, or how to find answers. Being lost is the absence of focus. It implies aimless wandering and confused direction.

The answer to feeling lost, therefore, is to figure out where to put our focus. As individuals and as a generation, we must set out to be focused, intentional, and specific in our pursuits.

We become lost in life when we take our eyes off the one true source of direction: God. Following his paths will keep us from being lost, just like following paths on a map. That's why having information at our fingertips doesn't guarantee that we won't get lost. We still have to follow the right paths and avoid aimlessly wandering off into the woods.

To state it even more clearly, our lives can only truly be founded in one thing, and that's the person of Jesus Christ. I'll discuss this more throughout the book, but Jesus really is the answer to life's biggest questions. Notice that I didn't say holiness is the answer or rules are the answer or the Ten Commandments or perfection. No, Jesus is the answer, and we must find our identity, our direction, and our value in him. When we do, we discover the desire and power to live healthy, whole, loving lives. But the transformation I mentioned above, the transformation that is often lacking in our generation, is not the result of religion but of relationship. It's not a product of legalism but of love.

After all, the Bible says Jesus came to seek and save the lost (Luke 19:10), which means he is pursuing you and me even more than we are pursuing him. He wants to be with us no matter how lost we are, and he wants to help us find our way back to his love.

If we fail to find ourselves in Jesus and fail to follow God's paths, the things of this world can steal our focus and divert our steps. That's precisely how we end up lost on so many of the wrong paths the world provides. But when we focus on Jesus, we find ourselves in him, and we stay on the paths God has paved for us.

I learned this the hard way. As I've mentioned, I was raised in a Christian family, and I knew about God and all the things he had done for me from an early age. But it turned out I was mostly living on my parents' faith, and I hadn't really given God his rightful place as Lord of my life. It's not that

I was outwardly rebelling, but I wasn't inwardly committed either—and that's just as bad, if not worse.

Eventually alcohol, girls, and popularity began to be a bigger part of my life than God. I still believed in him and knew Jesus had died for my sins and saved me by his grace and love, and I still went to church every week. But on the inside, I was lost.

God allowed me to do my own thing, wandering aimlessly along, for a couple of years. Then came a pivotal moment. I was sitting in the back of a small church in San Diego, listening to my dad preach, when a voice whispered in my head, *What are you doing?*

I knew God was speaking to me, and I was immediately overcome with fear. A healthy fear. I was faced with the fear of turning away from God—something I had heard my dad talk about many times.

In that moment, everything changed. I admitted the many things I had centered my focus on instead of God, and I acknowledged how much they had distanced me from my creator. I knew I had to make a change.

So I did. By the grace of God, and with a determination to act like the prince and coheir with Christ I knew I was called to be, I turned from the things that pulled my attention away from God and committed to giving him 100 percent of my focus. I got rid of *everything* that competed for my attention—even some things that weren't inherently wrong. But for me, in that season, I knew I needed a reboot. It was a time of radical recommitment, of turning my focus toward God and redefining my life and priorities as a result.

Through that process, I learned that it's not so much about *what* we are doing but more about if what we are doing is pushing us toward or away from God. That's important because, as I've said, being focused and found isn't about rules but about relationship. So rather than concentrating on what a "good Christian" does or doesn't do, learn what brings you closer to God. Learn what turns your heart toward Jesus. If you focus on him, you'll know how to live.

LOOK AROUND

Focusing on God is the key to enjoying everything else in life. Remember that hypothetical walk in the woods? The forest was beautiful, the vistas were breathtaking, the adventure was exhilarating . . . until they weren't. The beauty was real but being lost overshadowed everything. Now imagine if you hadn't experienced the fear, anxiety, and hopelessness of losing your way. What would your memories of that trip be? Nothing but awe and enjoyment.

In life, as in the forest, staying focused and found is the key to true adventure. Why? Because knowing where you are and knowing you are safe gives you freedom to explore and enjoy your surroundings. Life is an adventure that is best enjoyed when you are found, not lost; when you are safe on God's paths, not wandering aimlessly or desperately in circles. When you remain focused on Jesus and found in him, you have incredible freedom to experience life to the fullest.

Ask yourself this question: What things am I focused on right now and how do they affect my relationship with God?

Take a few minutes to really think about it before you answer. Maybe your answers are completely unique to you, but they may look a little like this:

- Building my relationships and spending time with friends
- Increasing my social media following
- Finishing my education
- Finding a spouse or significant other
- Strengthening my marriage or raising a family
- Chasing my dream job
- Reaching my fitness goals
- Participating in sports or hobbies

None of these are bad in and of themselves. In fact, they can all be gifts from God that add beauty and enjoyment to your life. But your eyes must be on him *first* or any of these pursuits can become unhealthy distractions.

Prior to the pivotal moment with God that I mentioned above, parties were a big part of my weekends. When I decided to refocus my life, though, I realized they were one of the pursuits that was distracting my attention, so I committed to staying away from them. That was a good decision, and I took it seriously. I was genuinely growing closer to God, and I was praying and thinking very seriously about what I was supposed to do with my life.

The following summer, however, I felt like God was telling me that it was okay to attend some parties again. Why? Because many of the people at those parties needed someone to speak truth into their lives. They were me before my San Diego wake-up call.

I set some boundaries to help me keep God as my focus, and I went to a few parties with a new purpose. I didn't focus on alcohol, drugs, girls, popularity, or acceptance. Instead

I simply asked myself, How can I love people in need? How can I help them know God?

I remember one party in particular. I noticed a girl across the room, and I felt a tug on my spirit that said, *Go talk to her.*

My first instinct was, *No way. Bad idea. I know what kind of reputation that girl has, and I don't want to get mixed up with that.*

But the tug came again and again. So somewhat reluctantly, I walked over and introduced myself. After about three minutes of incredibly awkward small talk, I said, "Hey, I just wanted to ask you, how are you doing?"

The conversation still felt uncomfortable, and I wasn't sure if I was doing anything right, but somehow that question brought her walls down. And with one sentence, I realized why God had sent me to that party. The girl looked at me with tears in her eyes and said, "Honestly, I told myself that if no one showed me any kindness tonight, I was going to kill myself after this party."

From that point on, every party I went to presented an opportunity for me to talk with someone about Jesus. I didn't force conversations to happen. I didn't push my agenda on anyone. I just showed up and encouraged people. I listened, I cleaned up vomit, and I got to watch as God transformed something that once turned my focus away from him into something I could use to point others to him.

In order to live a genuinely satisfying life—life as God designed it—you don't have to become a hermit and hide from the world forever. But it also doesn't mean becoming so immersed and absorbed by the world that you lose sight of God. It means keeping God first. It means making him your true north. It means focusing on him and enjoying every step, stage, vista, and adventure of this crazy journey we call living.

Stay aware of your surroundings—the people, the projects, the pursuits, the pleasures—without letting your surroundings pull you away from God. Enjoy them, explore them, and appreciate them. They are gifts from our creator, and as long as he is first, those things will take their rightful place.

And remember, you are called to a life that is bigger than just you. Be aware of the people around you. Part of your purpose—and our purpose as a generation—is to show others the love and acceptance we've found in God.

A CONFUSED NOISE

One of the things I love about our generation is that we want to make a difference. We are continually looking for ways to make an impact, to help social causes, and to promote justice. We want to do something that will affect a lot of people for good. We want our lives to matter.

Those are good, God-given desires. I think they reflect a divine calling on our generation.

When we help people, we are serving God. Jesus taught that when we show love and grace toward people in need, we are showing love to him (Matt. 25:40). He told his disciples that the entirety of Scripture can be summed up in two commandments: "love God" and "love others" (Matt. 22:37–40).

There is a problem, however. We often equate making "a difference" with "being noticed." In other words, we lose our focus. Instead of using our lives to make a difference for others, we begin to build our own fame and our own name.

We think the mark we make on our world rests on how many people know who we are or follow us on social media or listen to our opinions or ask for our advice.

Earlier we looked at the tower of Babel, which is a story about a group of people who took their focus off of God and instead tried to make life about themselves. The result was mass confusion. To this day, the term *babel* refers to "a confused noise made by a number of voices."[1] This story illustrated an important principle: *when a group of people have the wrong focus, confusion and chaos will result.*

We are a generation that wants to make a difference but also loves to be noticed, and that misguided focus is producing negative results. I think much of the confusion and emptiness that our generation expresses is a result of a collective focus on the wrong thing: on attention, on being noticed, on importance in the eyes of others. But just like in the story of the tower of Babel, an obsession with self will produce confusion and chaos.

God has called us to go out into the world, to spread his love, to share our knowledge of him, and to invite others to know God as well. If we refuse the call and hunker down in our little world instead, trying to build a name for ourselves by building some impressive tower that gets everyone to look at us, then we'll end up with the same results as Babel: the confused noise of many voices. When we focus on getting noticed, our minds become full of noise and confusion.

Like most people my age, the digital world is part of who I am, how I think, and how I work. So I'm not going to tell you that posting travel, food, or fashion pictures is egotistical or that blogging about your hobby or passion is dumb or that dating online is the wrong way to find love. Quite the opposite.

I believe social media, technology, and the internet are incredible tools to serve people and spread positive messages. But I do have a legitimate concern with their use. While a lot of good can come from social media outlets, blogs, and podcasts, these platforms have the potential to become breeding grounds for pride and comparison . . . and ultimately insecurity.

Who has the most followers? The most listeners? The most influence? Do people like what I post? Are they impressed with me? Do they envy me? Am I important? Do I matter?

The result of this frenzied pursuit for attention is confusion. We are confused about who we are, why we matter, what is important in life, and where we are going. Voices and opinions bombard us from all sides, and we don't know which ones to listen to.

This is a far bigger issue than social media, of course. The pursuit of self never ends well, regardless of the platform or medium. Why? Because we are not called to be famous; we are called to serve. We are not meant to focus on getting attention but to focus on God and his calling for us. The tendency to abandon our purpose in favor of attention is one we must resist in every area of life.

When we focus on loving God and loving others, the confusing voices are silenced. Life becomes simpler. The opinions and comments and labels of other people matter less. Our path becomes clear, and our focus keeps us from becoming lost in the clamor of confusing, noisy voices.

STUMPS AND ROOTS

I believe the desire to be significant is part of being human, because we all have a sense of calling and a need to matter.

So why does our desire for significance seem to so easily morph into a desire to be noticed?

Often it's due to a very simple, very common, and very unpleasant word: *pride.*

The story of Nebuchadnezzar, a great king of Babylon, is a clear illustration of this. It is found in the third chapter of the Old Testament book of Daniel. Nebuchadnezzar ruled an enormous world empire for many years.

That much power and influence can quickly go to someone's head, and in Nebuchadnezzar's case, it certainly did. One day, King Nebuchadnezzar decided to command his people to build a ninety-foot statue of himself. Then he ordered everyone in the kingdom to bow down in reverence to the statue whenever they heard the sound of trumpets.

Seems a little extreme, right? But how many of us go to great lengths to build ourselves up in the eyes of others? How much time do we spend trying to get noticed and make a name for ourselves? How much effort do we put into seeking people's praise and validation for our achievements? Sometimes without realizing it, we build our own idol of ourselves—often a digital one—and hope that people "worship" it.

Nebuchadnezzar's order was strictly enforced. Anyone who didn't bow to the statue would be thrown into a blazing furnace (probably one of the kilns that was used to make the statue itself). Three brave Hebrew men named Shadrach, Meshach, and Abednego refused to bow, preferring to trust God rather than pay homage to an idolatrous statue. They were promptly thrown into the furnace, but they were miraculously unharmed by the flames around them. The king, in amazement, noted that there were no longer three men in the fire but four—the God of Israel had come to the young men's aid. At that point, Nebuchadnezzar issued a new decree: if anyone spoke evil of God, their limbs would be ripped from their body. Clearly, Nebuchadnezzar was a man of extremes. Time passed, and soon he returned to his egotistical ways. One night he had a dream about an enormous tree that provided shelter and food for all the birds and wild animals. Suddenly, in his dream, a messenger from heaven ordered that the tree be chopped down and destroyed, but the stump and roots were to be left in the ground. At this point the dream began to focus on the person the tree represented, and the heart of that person was changed from the heart of a man to the heart of a beast.

The king was bothered by this dream, and he asked all of the royal advisers to interpret it. But adviser after adviser failed. Finally he asked his chief adviser, a Hebrew man named Daniel, for help.

When Daniel heard the dream, he was very troubled, but he explained its meaning. He said the tree represented Nebuchadnezzar himself and the massive kingdom he had built. The destruction of the tree meant the king would be driven from the palace and would live with the wild animals until he recognized that God is the one who gives power to the king. Eventually, just like a stump that grows into a new tree, Nebuchadnezzar would receive his kingdom back after being cut down.

The dream was a warning. God was reminding Nebuchadnezzar that his focus needed to be on God, not on his own name, his own fame, or his own power.

The Bible doesn't record whether the king made any changes to his life. But one year later, as he was walking on the roof of his palace, observing the vast expanse of his kingdom, his pride got the best of him again. He boasted:

Look at this great city of Babylon! By my own mighty power, I have built this beautiful city as my royal residence to display my majestic splendor. (Dan. 4:30 NLT)

While he was still speaking, a voice from heaven informed Nebuchadnezzar that his dream would now be fulfilled. The king essentially went insane, and just as Daniel had predicted, he was driven out of his palace and into the wild where he ate grass and lived like an animal for an extended period of time, possibly up to seven years.

Nebuchadnezzar's prideful ambition was his own undoing. When he lost his focus, he lost his mind.

Fortunately, the part of the dream that predicted his restoration also came true. In the dream, God specifically said to leave the roots and stump in the ground. He didn't rip them out and eliminate all hope for the king. Instead, he left a way for Nebuchadnezzar to return. And that's exactly what he did. Nebuchadnezzar admitted that God ruled over all the earth—including Babylon. He submitted his heart and pride to God. Just as he did when God saved Shadrach, Meshach, and Abednego, he looked up to the heavens and put his focus back on God. His sanity and honor were restored, and he was placed back upon his throne to lead his people.

God wants to see his people restored, and he always provides a way to return to him and his purpose for our life.

The stumps and roots are our way back home. I've seen in my own life the restoration power that comes when we return to where God planted us, when we turn our focus back to him in humility.

How about you? Is there an area of your life where you have let pride shift your focus from God to yourself or from serving others to serving yourself? And have you experienced loss as a result?

Maybe it's a loss of peace.

Maybe it's a loss of purpose.

Maybe it's the loss of a relationship.

Maybe it's the loss of a clean conscience.

Maybe it's the loss of closeness to God.

Whatever you might have lost, or however lost you might feel, there is a way back. God has not given up on you or me or on our generation.

His relationship with us is a covenant one: He has promised to be faithful to us and to love us no matter what. Regardless of how far we have wandered, he invites us to renounce pride and selfishness and renew our dependence on him.

COVENANT UNDERSTANDING

King David had an amazing understanding of God's covenant love for us. In Psalm 91, he describes God's attitude and commitment toward us when we focus on him.

> Because he has focused his love on me,
>   I will deliver him.
> I will protect him
>   because he knows my name.
> When he calls out to me,
>   I will answer him.

I will be with him in his distress.
I will deliver him,
and I will honor him.
I will satisfy him with long life;
I will show him my deliverance. (vv. 14–16 ISV)

David isn't saying that we should focus on God to earn his love; he's saying we should focus on God because he loves us. And because we keep our eyes fixed on him in faith and patience, God will care for us, protect us, and satisfy us.

Like a husband who vows to love his bride for better or for worse, for richer or for poorer, in sickness and in health, so God is committed to loving us. And just as a marriage covenant is mutual, we must be committed to him in the same way. That is the beauty of covenantal love.

God promises to never leave us or forsake us. In him, we will never be lost. We are the found, the chosen, the cherished.

Abandon distractions and give God your full focus. Keep your eyes on him, and the beautiful vistas and adventures of life will be all the more exhilarating.

WE ARE A **FOCUSED** GENERATION,
NOT A LOST GENERATION.
WE FOCUS ON GOD
AND WE FIND OURSELVES IN HIS LOVE.

THREE

BROKEN

The world breaks everyone and afterward many are strong at the broken places.

Ernest Hemingway

OUR GENERATION seems to be more aware of its brokenness, and of the brokenness of the world around us, than any generation before. We are surrounded by cynicism and criticism, by negativity and naysayers. The earth's resources are being depleted, injustice is rampant, prejudice and racism abound, epidemics and riots fill our news feeds.

There is more brokenness than ever, or at least we are more aware of it than ever, and it affects us deeply. We are consumed with thoughts of hopelessness and depression, and we have accepted anxiety as a way of life. Basically, we have come to believe that we are broken.

And no matter how many times we hear that we have more access and more potential than any generation before us, we still see our futures, our dreams, and ourselves as broken.

Maybe that's why I've become increasingly intrigued by the idea of brokenness. Not out of some morbid fascination with darkness, nor out of pessimism, but because I wonder what God will bring out of our brokenness if we let him.

We naturally assume brokenness is bad, because in many ways, it can be. For example, picture a flowerpot. The pot provides a place for flowers to flourish. It gives them protection and sustains their growth. That is what it was created to do.

If someone drops that flowerpot and it shatters to pieces, it no longer serves its purpose. Usually it is just swept up and thrown out. But that's not the only option for the broken pot. It could also be repaired, restored, and put back to use.

Those two options—*thrown out* and *restored*—are the same two options we face with the brokenness in our lives.

The first option, to be thrown out, illustrates being defeated. Defeat represents the times in life when we have no fight left in us. It seems like we have lost whatever battle we've been waging and there is no promise of victory on the horizon. It's over.

At times like this, we feel like we've fallen away from everything that is good and right. We've lost our purpose. What once was whole has now been shattered, and we don't have any confidence that we can put it back together.

A defeated brokenness brings hopelessness. If we are good for nothing but the trash pile, then why try? Why make good decisions? Why care about others? Why build for the future? Brokenness has a way of stealing our motivation and locking us into the present reality of hopelessness.

But it doesn't have to.

We can be restored. Rather than a *broken* generation, we need to see ourselves as a *restored* generation.

Restoration is the answer to brokenness. It negates the power of brokenness and erases its shame. It allows us to fulfill our original design and intent. A complete restoration is a triumph and a testimony.

The idea that we can be restored means three things: that there is hope in brokenness, that there is beauty in brokenness, and that there is victory in brokenness. The pieces of our lives have not been discarded and neither have those of our generation. Instead, we are being restored. We are being made into something stronger and more beautiful than ever, and our brokenness will ultimately be our victory. Let's look at each of these options for restoration in more detail.

HOPE IN BROKENNESS

Decades ago, when warhorses were trained for combat, they were first "broken." That is, they were taught to deny their instinct to run away from danger and instead taught to run directly into the line of fire. Once broken, a warhorse would no longer follow its natural instincts but instead would follow the will of the trainer who had broken it.

The same thing happens with broken *people*. The brokenness we have experienced (and continue to experience) often influences and controls our will. Instead of living in freedom, self-control, and wisdom, we end up putting ourselves in harm's way because something else is controlling us.

Maybe it's shame.

Maybe it's betrayal.

Maybe it's bitterness.

Maybe it's the loss of a loved one.

Maybe it's a shattered relationship.

Maybe it's the endless search for acceptance.

Maybe it's alcohol, drugs, or some other addiction.

The controlling influence is different for each of us, but the common denominator is that brokenness has allowed something or someone to gain a grip on us, and we are no longer in control of our own lives.

The principle is simple: The things that break us often control us.

The brokenness-creates-control dynamic can be direct or indirect. The thing that broke us might control us, or it might have created a broken environment that allows other things to control us.

For example, an abusive relationship is a form of direct control. If we are victimized, threatened, or abused by some-one, that person wields power over us with negative, danger-ous consequences. In that instance, we need more than just inner healing. We need to deal with our external situation immediately and decisively.

Most control is not that direct or literal though. Usually, it comes from a more hidden brokenness, one that began when a circumstance hurt us or frightened us, especially if it persisted over a length of time. Eventually, something broke in us: our hope, our faith, our self-esteem.

The loss of a loved one could exercise indirect control over us, because it might plunge us into depression or loneliness, which then deeply affects our emotions and lifestyle. The loss continues to control us, although indirectly, because there is a part of us that remains broken and susceptible to outside control—in this case, our emotions.

You can probably think of other examples. Repeated failure, perhaps in our careers or business endeavors, can break us. Financial losses or struggles can break us. Physical sickness can break us. Betrayal by a significant other can break us. A failed marriage can break us.

In your own experience, or perhaps in that of a loved one, you may have noticed how brokenness, control, and defeat seem to be cyclical. We feel broken, so we try to escape, but the escape itself is not healthy. Over time, our escape mechanism leaves us feeling even more defeated and broken, so we look for more ways to escape. In other words, because we don't deal with brokenness properly, we allow it to control us.

If control puts us at so much risk, why do we allow it to wield that much power in our lives? We give in to control because it's easier than dealing with the brokenness. Maybe it helps us escape suffering, at least temporarily. Or it helps us avoid owning up to our mistakes. Or it's the only alternative to confronting a toxic situation or an abusive person. We may allow ourselves to be controlled because we are afraid of even greater pain than what we've already experienced.

Most people would rather skip the pain of healing. They want to rush past the bad times and get to the good ones, and then pretend nothing ever happened. But doing so doesn't change the fact that the bad things actually occurred.

That is why it is important not to repress our pain or hide from our brokenness. Pain might be *repressed*, but it will never be *erased*. It's an authentic part of our life story. Instead of running *away* from the broken parts of our lives, we must run *toward* them. We must acknowledge them, process them, and heal from them.

That is called restoration, and the process starts with hope.

There is hope in the middle of our brokenness. We might feel like shards of clay that are shattered beyond repair, but that is not the case. Our pain is real, our brokenness is real—but so is our hope in God.

- He uses intended evil for our good. (Gen. 50:20)
- He makes grace abound where sin once ruled. (Rom. 5:20)
- He uses our weakness to show his strength. (2 Cor. 12:9)
- He creates beauty from ashes and turns tears to joy. (Isa. 61:3)

Where can we find lasting hope when we feel broken? In the restoration that God provides. In Jesus, our source of grace and hope.

There is hope in brokenness because God's love is greater than any tragedy, any pain, any loss, any abuse, any failure, any weakness, and any sin.

BEAUTY IN BROKENNESS

Kintsugi is an ancient form of Japanese art that highlights the beauty that can be found in brokenness. According to legend, kintsugi originated when a Japanese military commander broke one of his prized Chinese tea bowls and sent it off to China for repair. Upon its return, he discovered to his dismay that it had been fixed with large, bulky staples. He must have thought to himself, *There has to be a better way.*[1]

And there was. Japanese craftsmen found a way to repair broken pottery by infusing the cracks with a gold lacquer. The result was an art form that celebrates breakage and repair as part of the history of the object, rather than something to hide. The brokenness of an object doesn't mean the end of its story—instead, it's an essential part of it. Rather than hiding flaws, they are decorated with gold and crowned with significance. And not only does the repaired pot look better, it becomes more valuable.

In the same way, God infuses our brokenness with grace, and he makes us more beautiful than we were before. He puts our broken pieces back together and adds value to us in the process.

When we give God our brokenness, he infuses us with his life, and he covers our flaws with gold.

You may be thinking, "But Arden, you don't understand the brokenness I've gone through. God can't possibly use me." I don't pretend to know everything you've gone through. And I certainly would never minimize it. But I *do* know that Jesus was a master of using broken things. Think about this:

- The woman at the well was broken (John 4:1–26)
- The disciples Jesus called to join him in ministry were broken (Matt. 4:18–20)
- At the Last Supper, Jesus said, "This is My body which is *broken* for you" (1 Cor. 11:24 NKJV)

Regardless of your past and regardless of how broken you feel, there is power in the pieces of your past. There is beauty in your brokenness. There is greater value, greater joy, and greater influence ahead. When the transforming power of God is infused into your life, your brokenness becomes *more* beautiful. We've all gone through hardship and pain, and our natural instinct is to hide it. But I believe we should embrace it instead. It is part of our story and part of our testimony. We should become comfortable celebrating where we are now in relationship to where we were in the past. Our restoration is the story of God's love and grace, and it can bring inspiration to those who hear it.

VICTORY IN BROKENNESS

Our brokenness will actually be used for our good, not because of anything we do but because of the beauty and value that God places inside of us.

The Old Testament book of Judges covers a long, difficult stretch of Israel's history. Over the four hundred years covered in the book, Israel repeatedly turned away from God, which led to frequent defeat at the hands of their enemies. They didn't have a king, so God would raise up different individuals to be judges, or military leaders. These judges would save Israel, who would then follow God for a while, before turning away from him and facing defeat again. Talk about a vicious cycle.

The sixth chapter of Judges begins with one of the most memorable stories in the book—the story of Gideon. Not only is it a fascinating story but it also highlights the victory that is found in brokenness. And this story is certainly filled with broken things.

1. Israel Was Broken

The Israelites did evil in the eyes of the LORD, and for seven years he gave them into the hands of the Midianites. Because the power of Midian was so oppressive, the Israelites prepared shelters for themselves in mountain clefts, caves and strongholds. (vv. 1–2)

The Midianite army was massive, and they camped all around the Israelites, ruining their crops and killing their livestock. Israel was a broken nation that was hiding in the mountains, hoping and praying for restoration.

Keep in mind, the Israelites were in this mess because they had been worshiping foreign gods. They allowed their commitment to the one true God to be broken by idolatry, and eventually that broken loyalty led to brokenness and defeat as a nation. Remember, whatever breaks you ultimately controls you.

So, the Israelites cried out to God for help. God heard their broken cries and responded.

The angel of the LORD came and sat down under the oak in Ophrah that belonged to Joash the Abiezrite, where his son Gideon was threshing wheat in a winepress to keep it from the Midianites. When the angel of the LORD appeared to Gideon, he said, "The LORD is with you, mighty warrior." (vv. 11–12)

I love this because the angel spoke into Gideon's future. He gave Gideon a vision of restoration although Gideon had nothing to offer. In fact, at the time the angel appeared, Gideon was in hiding. He was threshing wheat in a winepress just to keep food hidden from the enemy. Some warrior. That brings me to the second broken part of this story.

2. Gideon Was Broken

In the middle of Gideon's mess, the angel told him to go in strength and save Israel out of Midian's hand. Like most of us would, Gideon responded by pointing out his brokenness and limitations.

> "Pardon me, my lord," Gideon replied, "but how can I save Israel? My clan is the weakest in Manasseh, and I am the least in my family." (v. 15)

Such a respectful argument, right? But the angel wasn't impressed. Look at the simplicity and power of his response.

> The LORD answered, "I will be with you, and you will strike down all the Midianites, leaving none alive." (v. 16)

In other words, "All the things that are oppressing you will be no more. Just trust me."

Gideon was still skeptical, but after some additional reassurances and a dramatic moment where fire came out of a rock and burned up his lunch, he was convinced. Mostly, anyway.

The first thing God asked of Gideon was to break down an altar to Baal, the false god Israel was worshiping. Inconveniently enough, God was asking him to break the altar

Gideon's own father had built. That brings us to the third instance of brokenness in Gideon's story.

3. The False Gods Were Broken

Gideon tore down a stone altar built for a false god, and in its place, he built an altar to the true God. He also cut down a wooden pole used for idolatrous rituals and used it as firewood to offer a sacrifice. He did all this at night, because he was afraid—but you have to give him points for creativity. His actions were a clear, in-your-face statement that the gods Israel had been worshiping were false, powerless . . . and broken.

The next morning, when the people noticed what had happened, they were upset and wanted to kill Gideon. But Gideon's father stood up for him, surprisingly. He told the people: "If Baal really is a god, he can defend himself when someone breaks down his altar" (v. 31).

Did you catch that? The man who built the altar seemed to recognize that Baal was powerless.

How often do the things that control us turn out to be powerless and broken themselves? We think that money is a secure place to put our faith, so we give our lives to building financial security only to discover that there is no lasting security in riches. Or we think our friendships matter most, and we do anything to win friends only to realize that they are just as broken as us.

Sometimes our brokenness helps us realize that the things we have trusted in—or the things that threatened us—are broken and powerless themselves.

Let that sink in—and then let the brokenness in your life point you back to God. He is the only infallible source of safety in this world. Yes, money and friends are necessary, along with many other things we pursue in life. But nothing can ever take the place of God. Giving control of our lives to something that is weak will only create more weakness. What is broken cannot make us whole.

The story didn't stop there though. After a series of conversations with God, and amid a lot of doubt in his own ability, Gideon summoned the people to battle, and thirty-two thousand showed up. That's when the story takes an unexpected turn.

> The LORD said to Gideon, "You have too many men. I cannot deliver Midian into their hands, or Israel would boast against me, 'My own strength has saved me.' Now announce to the army, 'Anyone who trembles with fear may turn back and leave Mount Gilead.'" So twenty-two thousand men left, while ten thousand remained. (Judg. 7:2–3)

God was basically saying, "If you win this battle with this big of an army, you'll think it's all about you. I need you to know that it was me who delivered you." So he reduced Gideon's odds by about two-thirds.

God's ways don't always make immediate sense to us, because he is God, and we are not. Going all in with him can be a scary decision. It requires us to trust even when the path God takes us on isn't clear, even when we are frightened, even when our family and friends don't understand, even when the odds are not in our favor. It's a plunge into the unknown!

God wasn't done preparing Gideon's army though.

But the LORD said to Gideon, "There are still too many men. Take them down to the water, and I will thin them out for you there. If I say, 'This one shall go with you,' he shall go; but if I say, 'This one shall not go with you,' he shall not go." (Judg. 7:4)

After God showed Gideon who was to stay in the army, he was left with a mere three hundred men to fight against an army whose warriors were too numerous to count.

Again, he was reminding Gideon that the battle would be won by God—not by human effort or strategy. God then gave Gideon the battle strategy which, of course, involved more brokenness.

[Gideon] returned to the camp of Israel and called out, "Get up! The LORD has given the Midianite camp into your hands." Dividing the three hundred men into three companies, he placed trumpets and empty jars in the hands of all of them, with torches inside. (Judg. 7:15–16)

The fourth and final broken aspect of this story of victory is this.

4. The Clay Jars Were Broken

The army, carrying torches hidden inside clay jars, reached the edge of the Midianite camp. On Gideon's signal, they blew their trumpets, broke the jars, and let the light shine through the broken pieces. The enemy was sent into total chaos and confusion. They turned on each other with their swords and either killed each other or fled for their lives.

I love the imagery of these broken men breaking the lantern jars. Think about it. Their broken jars released the fire that was inside. In the Bible, fire is a representation of the Holy Spirit. The broken jars paved the way for the Holy Spirit to bring victory in the middle of broken circumstances. Because of God's provision, the Israelites won a resounding victory over the enemy and delivered their people.

In the most unlikely circumstances, God used an underdog leader and a small band of warriors to defeat a massive army. A generation of defeated Israelites found hope in the midst of their desperation because God brought about victory through the trust of a broken man.

This is an important takeaway for us as we think about the broken pieces of our own lives.

HE'S NOT FINISHED

We, too, have become a broken generation. A generation raised, in many cases, without fathers or mothers. A generation of addiction. A generation of public violence and school shootings. A generation of climate change, of political unrest, of terrorist attacks, of pandemics, of racism.

And like the Israelites, we have often hidden from reality. We've strived to be unseen, to get by, to survive. We tried to escape pain, and in the process, we've often yielded control to someone or something else.

But God has not called us to simply "get by." Instead, he calls us to restoration, and he calls us to victory. Often, he uses our very brokenness to overcome the most challenging things that try to break us.

I don't know what you've been through, but I *do* know that God isn't done with you. He is calling you to be a Gideon to this generation. To bring hope to those who are tempted to give up. To stand up to insurmountable odds and face them without fear, knowing that God is on your side. To allow the Holy Spirit to work through broken people and broken stories. To restore what has been lost.

Whatever cracks you have, whatever brokenness you feel, God can use you to do mighty things, just like he did through Gideon. The world will tell you to hide your weakness and show your strengths. But we serve a God who can take our weaknesses and turn them into strengths (2 Cor. 12:9).

I've found that the more I give God my brokenness, the less it has control over my life. When people look at the parts of me that were once broken, they see Jesus and the work he's done in and through me. He has made me whole, and he can do the same for you.

Other people may see you as a shattered flowerpot, incapable of fulfilling a purpose, but God sees you as a vessel he can pour his Spirit into and shine his fire through.

The apostle Peter put it this way:

> And the God of all grace, who called you to his eternal glory in Christ, after you have suffered a little while, will himself restore you and make you strong, firm and steadfast. (1 Pet. 5:10)

Brokenness is never the end of your story; it's only the beginning. You can be restored. Your cracks will not be hidden but highlighted. God's grace will be etched in gold around the outlines of your weakness. You will become a restored vessel that serves as a testimony to God and his mighty work in your life. Instead of being broken, you will be restored to God's image and his calling for you.

WE ARE A RESTORED GENERATION,
NOT A BROKEN GENERATION.
OUR CRACKS ARE A STORY OF GRACE,
AND OUR LIVES ARE A TESTIMONY TO GOD'S LOVE.

FOUR

DOUBTFUL

Doubt is the incentive to truth and inquiry leads the way.

Hosea Ballou

THE FIRST SERMON I ever preached was on doubt. I was eighteen years old. I had just gone through a difficult season where I lost some friends in death and saw others sentenced to jail. I was doubting my faith and questioning why a God who loved me would allow so much pain in my life. But through that season, God showed me a side of doubt that I never knew before. The revelation I shared in my first sermon was deeply personal to me. It was something that, quite literally, changed my life.

As a teenager, I mostly coasted on my parents' faith. But a faith that wasn't *my own* wasn't strong enough to pull me through the painful valley of loss. So when uncertainties, questions, and skepticism stormed into my life, I was left with a choice: I could run *toward* God or *away* from him.

It's easy to assume that running toward God means running away from doubt. But I've learned that's not the case. Running toward God does not mean escaping our doubts and questions. It actually means embracing them and laying them down at God's feet. And in that process, we discover something: When we embrace our doubt, it becomes a catalyst for our faith.

Our faith needs challenges to grow. Think about plants that grow under extreme conditions, such as vegetation on the sides of cliffs, in deserts, or at high altitudes. These plants overcome hardship in order to grow. Despite windy or dry conditions or extreme temperature fluctuations, these plants flourish when faced with rough circumstances. In the same way, our faith will actually become stronger if we face the doubt, uncertainties, and fears that naturally occur in this crazy life.

If we never experience hard questions or feelings of uncertainty on our journey with God, there's a good chance we're not moving forward. We're not being challenged outside of our comfort zones. And we're not growing. An absence of doubt could indicate we are stagnant in our faith.

But that doesn't mean that growth is comfortable. The summer between seventh and eighth grade, I grew from 5'5" to 6'2", and I learned that growing pains are a real thing. I definitely felt uncomfortable as my body changed and developed. Sure, I was happy to get taller—but the struggle was real!

In the same way, the growth that is produced by doubt can be uncomfortable. But if we give up when we encounter discomfort and doubt, our roots will never go deeper.

How do we become a generation that learns to respond to doubts and questions in a healthy way? How can we be propelled forward by our skepticism and not held back by it? How can our uncertainties launch us into new levels of faith rather than uncontrolled spirals?

It starts with understanding this. Doubt is a clear indicator that God is setting us up for growth, and how we respond to doubt makes all the difference.

HIDE-AND-SEEK

Think about some of the reasons we might find ourselves dealing with questions and hesitations regarding our faith.

One reason for doubt could be *false information that contradicts God's character and his Word*. The world actively and frequently debates the truths we have received by faith through his Word. People deliver information or opinions that contradict the Bible with confidence and intelligence, and what they say can plant seeds of doubt in our hearts. *That is okay.* This kind of questioning can and should drive us to seek evidence. And if we seek evidence, we'll find the truth.

Another reason for doubt is *the instability of the world around us.* Our generation seeks stability because we have experienced so much change. The world is in constant flux. I think that plays a big role in fueling our uncertainties and reservations, because we don't know if what's here today will be gone tomorrow. But let's not let instability bring us to a standstill. Let's let it take us deeper into a relationship with God, into a knowledge of his Word, and into a life defined by wisdom.

Finally, doubt arises *when we face contradictory circum-stances*. In other words, when things don't make sense, when life doesn't work out like we planned, when God doesn't respond like we expected, or when beliefs we have held don't seem to be borne out in our day-to-day experience. These moments raise honest, gut-level questions—questions that need to be asked. They make us evaluate our philosophies of life, our assumptions about God, and our core values. Again, this is a good thing. The questioning is uncomfortable and even scary, but honest searching in the face of apparent contradictions will always produce growth when filtered through the lens of Scripture.

Doubt is a scary thing . . . until it isn't. It stops being scary when we decide to embrace it and engage with it, rather than hide from it or be embarrassed by it. We must decide to stop being a generation that is stuck in doubt and instead be a generation that pursues truth, searches for answers, asks hard questions, and finds real answers.

So what is the proper response to doubt? We will look at four options in this chapter, but they are all summed up in one word: *seeking*.

To seek means to pursue, to search, to explore, to chase, to follow, to investigate. Seeking is the opposite of hiding from our doubts or ignoring them. It is active, it is hope-filled, and it is courageous. When we seek answers, we acknowledge our uncertainties without being paralyzed by them. We engage the hard questions rather than giving up on them.

So let's seek God. Let's seek answers from his Word. Let's seek guidance from wise, God-honoring friends. Let's seek change. Let's embrace doubt so God can bring growth. Let's become known as a generation of truth seekers, not a generation of doubters.

Do you remember playing hide-and-seek as a kid? Think back to the thrill and the terror of hiding under a bed or in a closet, knowing the seeker was in the room, inches from your hiding place. And, on the opposite side, don't forget the determination, the frustration, and ultimately the triumph of looking for then finding someone who was hidden.

You will experience those emotions and more in your search for truth, so learn to enjoy the process. Don't resent the ambiguity. Don't fear the process of growth. Embrace the thrill, the uncertainty, the frustration, and yes, even the terror involved in seeking. Sometimes answers are hard to find, but the truth is there. You just have to look for it.

Remember, it's your journey and it's your search. You don't have to settle for rumors, feelings, assumptions, or other people's opinions. And don't let others criticize you for expressing skepticism about something or for questioning accepted conventions or for seeing things differently. Don't let your journey be dictated by someone else. Instead, go find out for yourself.

Yes, sometimes you need other people to guide, encourage, and shepherd you in your journey for answers. But it's ultimately up to you to navigate the process and direct your doubts toward faith. It's *your* journey.

Your research.

Your questions.

Your authenticity.

Your honest prayers.

Your creativity and logic.

Your curious, God-given mind.

Your discussions, debates, and decisions.

God is not afraid of your questions, and you shouldn't be either. Let God reveal himself to you as you bring your doubts to him. He knows that your natural response to uncertainty is confusion and fear. But he also knows what you can handle. And he believes in you! Your headfirst journey into doubt has the potential to reveal more of the beautiful, powerful faithfulness of God.

FOUR RESPONSES TO DOUBT

The four responses to doubt we will look at in this chapter all come from this idea of seeking, and they are illustrated in the lives of people in the Bible who, just like you and me, had to face contradictory circumstances and inner demons of doubt.

Learn like Solomon

When in doubt, seek wisdom and understanding.

King Solomon was an extraordinarily wise man, according to the Bible. He was also incredibly rich, successful, famous, and powerful. People came from all over the world to see his kingdom and learn from his leadership prowess. He wrote the bulk of Proverbs, as well as two smaller biblical books, Song of Solomon and Ecclesiastes.

The book of Proverbs is a collection of practical, down-to-earth advice for successful living. But more than that, it is a call to grow in wisdom and understanding. Solomon wrote:

> Get wisdom, get understanding;
> do not forget my words or turn away from them.

Do not forsake wisdom, and she will protect you;
love her, and she will watch over you. (Prov. 4:5–6)

Solomon didn't just want to give his readers advice, he wanted to inspire us to adopt wisdom as a lifestyle. He encouraged us to make the pursuit of understanding and knowledge a fundamental value in our lives. When doubt assails us, it should motivate us to become wiser, to gain understanding, and to grow in knowledge. Doubt should ultimately expand us. As we pursue answers, our minds, hearts, and worldview will grow bigger.

Chapter 8 of Proverbs is written in the first person, as if wisdom was a woman standing at a crossroads, reminding anyone listening to value growing, studying, learning, and understanding. Notice how this hypothetical messenger describes herself:

I, wisdom, dwell together with prudence;
I possess knowledge and discretion. . . .
Counsel and sound judgment are mine;
I have insight, I have power. (vv.12, 14)

In just two verses, eight different terms are used to describe the concept of learning. This proves that learning is a lot more than head knowledge. It's life knowledge. Solomon taught us that God wants you and me to be equipped to face the complexities of life. Our doubts and questions along the way should spur us to find answers.

If we look at the definitions of these terms in the original Hebrew language, we get a good panorama of the multifaceted learning that God wants us to experience.

- Wisdom: technical skill, experience, shrewdness
- Prudence: cleverness, discretion in practical affairs
- Knowledge: mental result of perception, learning, and reasoning
- Discretion: the trait of judging wisely and objectively
- Counsel: direction or advice for decisions
- Sound judgment: efficient, effective wisdom
- Insight: ability to understand
- Power: physically or mentally strong[1]

These are not discrete categories but overlapping terms that highlight the vastness and complexity of the learning process. Everything that happens to us can teach us; everything we face has the potential to make us grow.

We were created by God to grow in wisdom and understanding. We have the mental and emotional capacity to learn, adapt, and expand. This capacity is one of the greatest gifts humans have been given—but it's up to us to use it. We have to choose to be learners in the face of doubt.

Ask like Thomas

Learning is not the only response to doubt though. If you read Proverbs carefully, you'll find repeated references not just to learning new truth but to knowing the *source* of truth: God.

That brings me to a second response to uncertainty, skepticism, and hard questions: When in doubt, seek to know God better.

Most of us have heard the story of doubting Thomas, as he is often called. He's the classic example of someone who expressed doubt. Thomas wasn't with the rest of the disciples when Jesus first appeared to them after the resurrection. And when they shared with him what had happened, Thomas didn't believe them. He needed to see Jesus for himself as proof of the resurrection.[2]

Thomas has often been criticized for his doubts, but I can relate to him all too well. And to be honest, I love what Thomas's story teaches us. Instead of turning away from Jesus based on the doubts he felt, or hiding his skepticism and pretending to be okay, Thomas put it all out there and proclaimed, "I need to see you, Jesus!"

Ideally, Thomas would have just believed without seeing. But he couldn't. And he was too intellectually honest to fake it or ignore his questions. He gave himself permission to doubt. And when he did, the most amazing thing happened: Jesus showed himself to Thomas in response.

Jesus didn't yell at him or rebuke him. He didn't mock him or kick him out of his group. He gave Thomas the proof he needed, then gently said, "Stop doubting and believe" (John 20:27).

I believe God has the same response to our genuine doubts. He cares about them. He understands them. He's patient with them. He goes out of his way to address them. And then, when we are ready, he invites us to believe in him. Just like Thomas, the answer to our doubts isn't just information: it's a person. It's Jesus.

Notice that there's a difference between "believing" and "believing *in*." Thomas had always *believed* Jesus. He had walked with Jesus and seen the amazing miracles that Jesus performed. He *believed* that Jesus was the Son of God. But he didn't *believe in* Jesus's ability to defeat death and be resurrected from the tomb until he saw the evidence himself.

If we continue to follow Thomas's life story as told through Christian history, we discover that the guy we know as a doubter became one of the most faith-filled men in history. In fact, he left everything that was familiar to him and traveled to India to preach the gospel. He was eventually martyred for his faith. The person he once doubted became the person he gave his life for. That is the power of proven faith.

Thomas's life shows us that doubt isn't the end of our faith; often, it's the beginning of a great journey. It could be argued that without the doubt that Thomas experienced—and his willingness to express that doubt and find answers to it—he never would have impacted the world the way he did.

Thomas came to know Jesus in a new way through his questions and his skepticism. He met him not just as a teacher or a mentor or a friend but as God. The power of God was proven to Thomas in the person of Jesus, and that mindset shift happened in response to his doubt-filled questions.

Thomas shows us that we shouldn't just disregard our doubts. People have told me to ignore my doubts and just have faith. To be honest, I've probably told myself that at times. But that's not how it works. Just like pain, doubts cannot be buried in our hearts. Questions will inevitably come up—big ones and little ones. No matter how much we try to suppress them, they don't just go away.

Author Gary R. Habermas describes the confusion surrounding doubt and faith this way:

> Few subjects are characterized by more misunderstandings than this one. Contrary to popular opinion, doubt is not

always sin. Neither is it necessarily the opposite of faith nor the product of weak faith. It is experienced by many believers in Scripture, such as Abraham, Job, David, Jeremiah, and John the Baptist. And almost all believers, as well as unbelievers, experience doubt at times. As strange as it seems, doubt can produce positive results, and many doubters are very much in love with the Lord.[3]

The stories of Abraham, Job, David, and other biblical heroes illustrate the same truth Thomas experienced: fear and doubt, when processed correctly, can lead to greater faith. That's why, throughout the Bible, we read about God telling his people to "fear not" and to believe instead of doubt. Not because fear and doubt can easily be dismissed but because God knows how we are wired. He understands that our first response to trials and adversity is to feel anxiety and uncertainty. He also knows, though, that those things are not the end of our story. We should not ignore our doubt, but we shouldn't wallow in it forever either.

Instead of denying our doubts and viewing them in a negative light, I want us to see them as something that can actually take us deeper into our relationship with God. As we develop the ability to acknowledge our doubts instead of allowing them to haunt our minds and weigh us down, we'll become comfortable with confronting them and taking them to God.

When I first felt called into ministry, I feared that my doubts disqualified me from my calling. I concluded, like Habermas mentions, that because I doubted, my faith was weak. I assumed other pastors, authors, and speakers never asked questions about their faith.

I remember one day in particular when I was feeling overwhelmed by doubt. I sat down at my desk and pleaded with God, *Lord, I don't know why this is happening to me. But if I can get through this, I can get through anything.* In that moment, my shame turned to resolve. Instead of being afraid of doubt, I decided to tackle it head-on.

I started reading books about the character of God and how great people responded to doubt and hardship in their lives. My goal was to search for deeper truth that I could sink my teeth into. That's when I found myself immersed in the life of the Old Testament character of Job, who we'll look at in the next section. I discovered that many of the greatest Christian leaders in history experienced doubt—probably *all* of them.

Charles Spurgeon, one of the best communicators of truth of all time, said this:

> I think, when a man says, "I never doubt," it is quite time for us to doubt him, it is quite time for us to begin to say, "Ah, poor soul, I am afraid you are not on the road at all."[4]

In other words, if you have doubts, you are in good company! People like Abraham and Thomas and Charles Spurgeon have gone before you, and they are leading the way. Not toward mere facts but toward the person of Jesus and a deeper walk with God.

When doubts assail you, find God in them. Look for Jesus in the midst of the storm. He is walking on the waters of fear and uncertainty alongside you. Come to know God in his power, his love, and his grace. Like Thomas, see the reality of Jesus, crucified and risen again, present with you, proving himself and assuring your heart.

When you do, doubt will become relationship, relationship will become faith, and faith will become victory.

Trust like Job

I mentioned earlier that the story of Job meant a lot to me during my personal journey of doubt. Job is known for his suffering, for his complaints, for his patience, for his remarkably nonempathetic friends, and ultimately for his restoration. But the primary message of the book actually isn't about Job at all. It's about God.

That brings me to a third response when we are confused, doubting, and uncertain: When in doubt, seek to trust in God's sovereignty.

Before I explain what I mean, let's take a brief look at Job's story. It begins with an affirmation by God that Job is a righteous, upstanding, exemplary person. He trusts and obeys God, and God seems very proud of him.

That makes what happens next even more confusing.

The enemy obtains God's permission to test Job. First, all of Job's cattle are stolen or killed. This includes oxen, sheep, donkeys, and camels—a huge financial loss for Job.

But it's nothing compared to what happens next. Job's ten children are feasting and celebrating at the oldest brother's house when a powerful wind sweeps through, causing the house to collapse and kill all ten children.

On top of that, Job is struck with a terrible disease which strips him of both his health and his dignity. His body is covered in painful sores, and he is in constant misery.

Finally, adding insult to injury, Job's closest friends lash out at him, implying that all of this misfortune is his own fault. He must have sinned, they assume, because otherwise he would not be suffering like this. Job's wife takes another approach: she tells Job to give up, curse God, and die. Not exactly encouraging.

It's fascinating to see the ups and downs in Job's response to his pain. He lost everything: his family, his belongings, his dignity, his hope. Yet his first response revealed the strength of his devotion to God. He said, "The LORD gave me what I had, and the LORD has taken it away" (Job 1:21 NLT). He seemed calm and unshakable.

Over time, however, Job's language changed, and it became clear that doubt flooded his heart and mind—and understandably so. He questioned God's wisdom in even allowing him to be born in the first place.

In response, God revealed himself to Job quite dramatically: he spoke from the eye of a violent storm. For three chapters, God probed Job with questions.[5] Questions that began to stir his doubt into faith. Questions like, "Why do you talk without knowing what you're talking about?" and "Where were you when I created the Earth?"

God wasn't antagonizing Job with these questions. He was revealing his own greatness and showing Job that humans are limited in their opinions and interpretations of life circumstances.

There are two things to notice here. First, as he did with Thomas, God took the time to address a doubting human. He didn't ignore Job or reject him, although he did call him out a little for his self-righteous attitude.

Second, though, God didn't explain himself. He never told Job that the devil was trying to get him to renounce God. He simply said, "Job, I'm God, and you're not, so stop talking and just trust me."

When the king of all kings turned his attention to a person and opened his mouth, it was awe-inspiring. Job is overwhelmed. Here's how he responds:

> I'm speechless, in awe—words fail me.
> I should never have opened my mouth!
> I've talked too much, way too much.
> I'm ready to shut up and listen. (Job 40:3–5 MSG)

But God wasn't done. For two more chapters, he emphasized his sovereignty and wisdom. He reminded Job that he didn't have to explain himself. Job replied with another statement of humility:

> I admit I once lived by rumors of you;
> now I have it all firsthand—from my own eyes and
>   ears!
> I'm sorry—forgive me. I'll never do that again, I
>   promise!
> I'll never again live on crusts of hearsay, crumbs of
>   rumor. (Job 42:5–6 MSG)

Just like Thomas, Job found God in the midst of doubt. He admitted that his prior knowledge was based on rumor and hearsay, but then he came to know God for himself.

But Job also received a lesson in humility and trust, and it's a lesson we need to take to heart as well. God graciously reveals himself to us, but he is not obligated to explain his every move. And we don't have the right to tell him how to do his job. When doubts and questions fill our minds, we need to remember who God is and who we are, and we need to trust God more than ourselves.

The story of Job reveals God's sovereignty, but that doesn't mean it's a story of a tyrannical God imposing his arbitrary will on helpless subjects. Far from it. The story is a clear illustration that God uses his power for our good. Yes, he is sovereign, but he is also loving. Both of those things work together, and they allow us to trust him no matter what circumstances we might face.

One last note: it's interesting how quickly and confidently Job's friends assumed that his pain was his own fault. Job was being tested because of his faithfulness, but he was condemned by his friends because of his circumstances. We must be careful not to assume that our circumstances are always a result of God's correction. When bad things happen, we often have a tendency to think God must be punishing us for something we've done. But when we put our trust in Jesus Christ, our past, present, and future sins are forgiven. God doesn't hold them against us, and he doesn't make us pay for them.

When you face contradictory circumstances or difficult questions, trust in God's sovereignty and goodness. You don't have to have an explanation for everything, you don't have to understand everything, you don't even have to control everything. Like Job, let doubt turn you toward trust, and remind yourself that God is still in control.

Look for Peter

I want to close this chapter with a story that's very personal to me: partly because of the emotions surrounding it and partly because of what I learned through it. But first, let me give you the fourth and final response to doubt I want us to consider: When in doubt, seek to recognize what God is doing.

My story begins on a plane. My coworker and I were about to take off for a conference. Once on board, we met a mother and her brother who were traveling with the woman's terminally ill daughter. My coworker initiated a conversation with them, and we learned that this trip was part of their faith efforts to find healing for the young girl. My coworker offered a beautiful prayer for the family, while I found myself asking God what words could be of encouragement in such a dark, desperate situation.

As the plane took off, I put on my headphones and hit shuffle on my worship playlist. A song called "As It Is in Heaven" by Hillsong began playing. As I listened, a couple of phrases captured my attention. The narrator of the song talks about singing "with no sickness in my body" and "like no prison walls can hold me" because we know that we are free.[6]

When I heard those words, I knew they were for this family. Even in this time of brokenness, they could sing like there was no sickness in the young girl's body, like no prison walls could hold her, like she had been set free.

After the flight landed, I found the family and encouraged them to hold on to the promise in those words and trust God for their daughter's healing. I shared a prophetic word and prayer over her before heading off to the conference with a promise that I would keep in touch.

And for the next few months, I continued to follow up with that family to get updates on the daughter's condition.

No immediate improvements seemed to take place. But I maintained a high level of faith that good things were going to happen.

Months went by, and things remained the same. Then one day I was blindsided by news of the daughter's passing. It hit me like a ton of bricks, and I spiraled into a state of sadness and depression. I remember praying many times, *God, what happened? You gave me the song, I heard you speak, I did what you asked me to do, and now she's gone.*

I didn't talk about it with anyone. Honestly, I felt guilty. I had been sure God was going to heal this girl. And when it didn't happen, I chalked it up to weakness in my own faith. Her passing was evidence that I didn't pray hard enough. That I had too much doubt.

I remained in this state for over a month. Finally, one day at the gym of all places, I remember asking God yet again, *Why didn't you heal her?*

I felt him prompt me, *Listen to the song again.*

So I did—several times—but it still didn't make any sense to me. *God, you said that she would sing like a person with no sickness in her body, with no prison walls that would hold her. I don't get it!*

Then suddenly, as if for the first time, I noticed the first words of the song: "Whether now or then . . ." The lyrics point to how we can live here on earth today because of what we know will be true in heaven.

Coincidentally, I had just read a story in Acts 12 about Peter being imprisoned for preaching. The chapter details how his fellow believers gathered in a house to intercede on his behalf. They prayed and believed that Peter would be set free. Miraculously, an angel appeared to Peter, rescued him from prison, brought him out into the street, and then disappeared.

Peter went to the house where all the believers were gathered and knocked on the door. A servant girl answered, and in her amazement, left him standing outside while she ran back inside to tell everyone, "Peter—you know, the guy you're praying for—is at the door!"

Their reply? "You're crazy! He's not at the door. He's in prison. Now leave us alone so we can pray for him to be set free." That's my paraphrase, but it's pretty close to the actual account. Here was a group of people praying fervently, and their miracle literally showed up at the door, and they didn't even recognize him.

That day at the gym, the story of Peter and my confusion about the girl I was praying for came together as two aspects of the same truth. I finally realized what God was saying to me. *Arden, I didn't give you that song just as words from you to her. That song is her testimony to you and everyone else: "Like no prison walls can hold me, I will sing like I am free." You've been praying and believing that she would be healed, and she is! She is whole, and she is with me. She's in paradise. The miracle is done, it's standing on your doorstep, but you haven't realized it.*

I don't know how to fully explain it, because the pain of the loss was still there, and even many of the doubts, but I saw so clearly that in the midst of my doubts, my pain, my loss, and my fear, God was at work.

He is always doing something. He is always working miracles. He is always answering prayers. It may not look like we expect it to, but let's not miss what he is doing. Let's not leave the answer standing at the door.

We've all experienced difficult circumstances or tragic news. Maybe we even prayed intensely and believed deeply but God didn't respond the way we thought or believed he would, which led to more doubts and questions. Life can be a roller coaster of emotions, of doubt and confidence, of questions and answers, of waiting and prayers. But regardless of our feelings, God is always faithful, and regardless of what we can see or not see, he is always at work.

In my case, I went through a season where I heard God speak and was excited about what was going to happen. And then I went through a season of doubt because things didn't turn out the way I thought. Even though I didn't recognize God's faithfulness during that time of doubt, he was still working from the moment he spoke to me. And he did bring the healing I was so confident he'd promised. It just came in a different way than I imagined or wanted.

No matter what doubts you feel right now, know that God is at work. Learn to look around, to see with God's eyes, and to recognize his hand in your life.

Maybe you need wisdom like Solomon. Or a revelation of Jesus like Thomas. Or to trust in God's sovereignty like Job. Or an awareness of your miracle like the friends of Peter.

Wherever you are at, whatever your doubts might be, you can seek and find the answers you need. Don't be afraid. Don't be ashamed. Take your doubts to God, and let your faith grow.

WE ARE A SEEKING GENERATION,

NOT A DOUBTFUL GENERATION.

WE EMBRACE QUESTIONS,

WE CHALLENGE ASSUMPTIONS,

AND WE FIND OUR TRUTH IN GOD.

FIVE

REGRETFUL

The only people with no hope are those with no regrets.

Michael Hyatt

WE'VE ALL EXPERIENCED the feeling of helplessness that comes from regret. It follows that decision you made that you wish you hadn't or the decision you *didn't* make that you wish you had. It's the unshakable agony of not being able to change the past.

Most of us know that we shouldn't let regret steal our joy. Yet I wonder how many of us know that the danger isn't actually within regret itself. The real issue arises when a shoulda, coulda, woulda mentality festers in our minds and leaves us more frustrated, bitter, and cynical than we were before we messed up.

My goal for this chapter is to change how we approach regret and to learn how we can use it to our advantage.

The word *regret* does not have to have a negative connotation in our lives. It simply means to feel sadness or disappointment over past actions. Related terms include remorse, sorrow, contrition, and repentance.

Most of us would assume regret is a negative emotion simply because it stems from a mistake or failure, but that doesn't mean that regret itself is wrong any more than the pain we feel when we smash our thumb with a hammer is wrong. Just like a throbbing thumb, the pain of regret exists to alert us to danger and motivate us to be more careful in the future.

I'm sure we've all had one of those "what was I thinking?" moments—probably many of them. Just reliving those memories can make you squirm a little, although with the passage of time, we're often able to look back at them with humor.

- The bowl cut our mom gave us when we were young
- The crash-and-burn we had the first time we asked someone out
- The pivotal mistake we made that lost the big game for our team

Those are the kinds of things that, years later, we can laugh and joke about. But there are other mistakes that become dark secrets, things we keep hidden out of shame and remorse. The problem is, those hidden things have a way of holding us back.

During high school, I made a lot of choices that I later regretted. For a long time, I held on to those regrets and let them control me. They affected my relationship with God, my prayer life, my willingness to serve in the church, my thought life and emotions, and my other relationships.

As I grew in my walk with God, he gave me wisdom and discernment to make better choices. But the regret of my past mistakes still haunted me. Why had I put myself in those situations? Why didn't I know better? Even though God was propelling me forward, I felt like regret was keeping me anchored to my past.

Fast-forward a couple years to when I started working for my parents in ministry. While I didn't realize it at the time, I did a lot of things during my first year there that lost people's trust. On many occasions I took days off work to go hang out with friends, even when I knew I was needed on the job. I fell asleep at my desk multiple times. I sent rude emails to team members rather than having mature conversations. I reported negative information to my parents without following the right chain of command. They were small things in the moment, but they added up.

It wasn't until I stepped out of my role and took a year off that I realized what I had done. Outside perspective brought a lot of clarity, and that's when the regret came flooding in. Those same emotions that had followed my wrong choices from high school surfaced again. But this time they carried even more weight, because when not addressed correctly, regrets gain momentum with every new mistake. Now, not only was I still asking the familiar question of "how could I have done that?" but I also started thinking, *Am I even capable of being in ministry?* and *Who am I, really?*

I had allowed regret to disrupt my future because I didn't handle the problems of my past. I focused on my regret for too long, and it rendered me inactive.

Regret is often confused with guilt or conviction. But they're not the same. Guilt *condemns*, conviction *rebukes*. Prolonged regret does neither. It *immobilizes*.

Ironically, regret is something that should produce an immediate response. Maybe it's an apology, a change of heart, offered forgiveness, an ended relationship, or a modified behavior. If we refuse to take appropriate action based on what regret is telling us, we'll remain immobilized by it. And we'll commit the same mistakes over and over.

After a year of living in my own mental tug-of-war, God showed me that if I handled regret correctly, it could actually propel me even further. He gave me a vision for my future that I knew I could only reach by letting go of my past. He allowed me to see glimpses of who I was and who I was becoming. He gave me a vision for my future that did not include carrying my past regrets. I felt like he was saying, *Arden, there's too much to do. There's no room for wallowing in your past.*

So I repented to God, my parents, and my coworkers. Everyone was gracious toward me, and I was blessed to be welcomed back on the team after a year away. But I didn't bring my old ways with me this time. I refused to let my past slow down my present—both by choosing not to live in regret and by changing the behavior that caused that regret in the first place.

That's where regret began to help me. It was not a regret that I carried with me though. I had dealt with the shame and guilt of my former mistakes, and I had left the immobilizing aspect of regret in the past. But I still remembered it, and I had a healthy respect for its effect on my life. I knew the pain of poor choices. I knew the shame and remorse of wrong actions.

Regret narrowed my focus and highlighted the course I wanted to follow. I had a vision for my life before, but I was too immature to see it clearly or to value it enough. Now, however, I was developing enough humility to learn from my mistakes. My regrets helped me see what needed to change.

Regret can either rob us of our future or propel us into it. The choice is up to us.

Embracing regret can feel as if we're admitting failure or abandoning faith. But in reality, it means that our hearts are sensitive toward whom we are becoming. Godly distress over our mistakes will drive us straight into our Father's arms. When we repent, and when God washes us with his radical grace and forgiveness, we can lift our heads high, turn in a new direction, and live victoriously. It can become a beautiful part of his redemption story in our lives.

THIS ONE'S ON ME

The first thing we must do to grow through regret is take personal responsibility for our actions. That's the whole point of regret, after all: to indicate our mistakes and motivate our change. We must have the courage and honesty to say, "I blew it. This one's on me. I'm sorry. I'll do better next time."

I love the way 2 Corinthians 7:10 reads in *The Passion Translation*.

> God designed us to feel remorse over sin in order to produce repentance that leads us to victory. This leaves us with no regrets. But the sorrow of the world works death.

Notice the positive progression:

Mistake → Remorse → Repentance → Victory

There is a negative progression listed here as well:

Worldly sorrow → Death

When we make wrong choices, we have the power to reverse course. But the outcome depends on the way we process the regret that stems from our mistakes. If we blame others, play the victim, or wallow in our grief but never own up to what we did, we miss the opportunity to capitalize on our mistakes. That is worldly sorrow, and it produces death. Death of our future, of our relationships, of our calling, of our self-esteem.

If, however, we repent—if we accept that no one is to blame but ourselves and recognize where we went wrong—then regret becomes a powerful tool. Godly remorse for our actions motivates us to go a different direction moving forward. The positive progression starts with accepting personal responsibility, and the result of that choice is life and victory.

THIS ONE'S ON THEM

It's easy to say we should accept responsibility for our mistakes, but what about regret that is tied to actions that have been *done to us*? What happens when we feel grief and regret over something when we were the victims? Maybe it was a betrayal or acts of abuse or rejection or deceit.

This sort of regret brings with it a storm of emotions, and it's difficult to process for two reasons. First, because we have no control over other people, so we can't force them to acknowledge their mistakes or make things right. And second, because we often feel partly to blame. That's what regret does—it points out blame for the sake of change. So we often don't know who to blame, what to fix, or how to move on. It's complicated, and it hurts.

On one hand, I want to say very clearly that you don't have to carry guilt for what someone else did. Regret is about accepting personal responsibility, so if you didn't make the mistake, you can't take the blame. Doing so is not healthy or honest, so give yourself permission to move on from past hurts. If you are dealing with feelings of this nature and you've been unable to shake them, consider seeking professional counseling. You deserve to live free from shame from other people's violence or carelessness toward you.

On the other hand, there are many circumstances where both parties are at least partially at fault. In those cases, regret is the stimulus you need to figure out what you did wrong and attempt to remedy it. Don't accept 100 percent of the blame if the other person did something wrong as well, but do let regret produce repentance for the part you played in the mistake. Then leave the past behind and move forward into peace.

I'm not a psychologist, so I'm not trying to unpack the complex nature of hurt, resentment, and guilt. But I am *human*, just like you, and I've experienced my share of hurts and regrets too. The collision of emotions in our hearts can threaten to throw everything off balance, and it's important that we learn to walk through sorrow and regret the way God intended, in a way that brings life instead of death.

USE REGRET THE RIGHT WAY

There are two strong emotions that tend to accompany regret, whether it's for our own actions or for those of others.

First, we often feel deep *sadness*. There is a sense of loss, a feeling that something was taken from us, or a realization that we were made to suffer, and those emotions create sorrow. Second, we often feel *anger*. The loss or suffering we experience stirs up resentment. We want revenge and we want justice. We want someone else to feel the hurt we have felt.

Unfortunately, to deflect our pain and strong emotions, we often look for something or someone else to blame. Rather than allowing our regret to awaken a sense of personal responsibility, we go into protective overdrive, frantically searching for something to make us feel better. We replay past wrongs over and over until we feel justified in the poor choices we made. We fixate on the past, almost irrationally. We waste time, energy, and emotions on things that are over and gone. As a result, we can't seem to move on.

But here's the truth: we can't change the past. As much as we wish we or someone else had done something different, that's not an option. The only thing we can change now is our present; and by changing our present, we can change our future. The key to finding healing and moving forward is not rationalizing, ignoring, or rewriting the past; it's accepting where we were wrong and making real changes as we look toward the future.

Again, I'm not attempting to minimize or criticize past trauma. That would be incredibly presumptuous of me. Your story is your story, and I can't speak for you. But what I can tell you is that even in your pain, even in my pain, God has a future for each of us. We don't have to live under the power of worldly sorrow that produces death. Instead, we can let godly *remorse* point us toward practical *change* and ultimately experience *victory* over our mistakes.

So what does our generation need in order to move forward from regret? We need courage, honesty, and humility to take responsibility for ourselves, our past actions, our present mindsets, and our future choices.

I believe that these three things—courage, honesty, and humility—are the natural result of gaining understanding and awareness. That's why I've focused so much on the need to face the past, not hide from it. When we shine a light on whatever it is that we feel regret for, we become empowered to make positive change.

Therefore, the word I want to use to counteract regret is *awakened.*

We are not to be a regretful generation, who lives under the cloud of past mistakes. No, we need to be an awakened generation.

Our awakening must come through regret though. That is a key point here. We can't avoid mistakes, but we can learn from them.

To help us understand this truth, I want to look at the story of someone in the Bible who dealt with a massive amount of regret: King David. His life illustrates several principles of awakening through regret that are very applicable to our generation today.

WHEN KINGS MAKE MISTAKES

King David is one of the greatest figures in the Bible. He was a noble man, a great king, and someone who truly followed and reflected God's heart, even in the midst of his regrets.

We can read about one of his greatest regrets in 2 Samuel 11–12. One evening, while walking about the rooftop of his palace, David looked out and saw another man's wife, Bathsheba, bathing. A little situational awareness would have been helpful here. But instead of looking away and going about his business, David made one of those "what was I thinking?" decisions. He ordered the woman to come to his palace, and he used his status as king to get her into bed.

Some time passed, and then Bathsheba sent word that she was pregnant with David's child. David panicked. Her husband was off at war, fighting for the king and putting his life at risk for his nation, so people were going to find out it wasn't his baby.

Rather than owning up to his mistake, David tried to hide it. He brought Bathsheba's husband, Uriah, home for a visit. He assumed Uriah would sleep with his wife, and everyone would assume the child was his. Boom, problem solved. What could go wrong?

But Uriah wouldn't even sleep in his house. Not because he didn't love his wife but because he refused to enjoy the comforts of home while his fellow soldiers were still in the throes of battle. His moral strength and clear values stood in stark contrast to David's behavior.

David was stuck in a downward spiral of regret and cover-ups, and he tried to cover his tracks once again. He called Uriah to the palace and got him drunk, hoping he'd lower his guard and go home to his wife. But that didn't work either.

Finally, David sent Uriah back to battle and ordered his general to intentionally put him in harm's way. Uriah died defending his king, and after an appropriate period of mourning, David married the widowed Bathsheba, and she gave birth to their son.

It's a terrible story of abuse of power, lies, cover-ups, and violence. From start to end, David's actions were reprehensible. I'm sure he battled some emotional aftermath and regret for his actions, but it seems like he thought that he'd successfully covered up his bad decisions without consequences.

He was wrong.

Sometime later, God sent a prophet named Nathan to expose David's wrong decisions. Nathan told David a story about two men: one rich, one poor. The rich man had many sheep. The poor man owned just one, and it was very precious to him. In the story, the rich man stole the poor man's sheep.

David was infuriated by the injustice of the story. But then Nathan dropped the hammer. David was the man who "stole the sheep" when he took Bathsheba from Uriah.

David finally recognized that he had messed up. He owned up to it, and that's when reality set in for the king.

I equate this moment in David's life to what I experienced during my year off from ministry. It reminds me of the time when having an outside perspective showed me all the ways I had broken people's trust. When I finally took an honest, humble look at my past behavior, the flood of regret was instantaneous.

After Nathan confronted him, David cried out in repentance, "I have sinned against the Lord!" (2 Sam. 12:13). He showed godly remorse for his actions and poured out his heart to his heavenly Father. He wrote Psalm 51 during this time, and the depth, honesty, and rawness of his emotion is clear.

David could have blamed someone else or let his pride drown out his remorse or ignored godly counsel. He could have just said, "Yes, I did it, but I'm the king. The kingdom and everything in it are mine, and I can do whatever I want." And in that ancient culture, he probably could have gotten away with it.

Instead, he humbled himself, cried out to God, and reset the course of his future.

Here's the reality: we can't change what we've done, but we *can* change our future through repentance. For that to happen, we have to go through an awakening. We have to experience a raw, humble awareness of what we have done wrong that can lead us to authentic change.

It took David a long time to reach that moment of awakening, unfortunately. In the meantime, he compounded his error many times over. You and I face the same choice: Will we hide and ignore the past? Will we pile mistake upon mistake in an attempt to bury our failures? Or will we allow regret to awaken us?

This story reveals six areas that need to be awakened in each of us as we deal with our mistakes. They are painful—I'm not going to lie—but they are necessary, and they will ultimately lead to grace, life, and victory in Christ.

Awakened to Our Faults

We are going to mess up and hurt people. I hate to say it, but it's true. None of us are perfect. That doesn't mean we can excuse our mistakes, but it does mean we can expect them.

We learn from David how difficult it is to accept blame. He was clearly in the wrong. No one can read his story and justify his actions. Yet his shame, pride, and guilt hindered him from fully seeing the truth until the prophet Nathan pointed it out to him.

Similarly, it is natural for us to resist admitting our mistakes. Be aware of that tendency and don't let it blind you. It's a self-defense mechanism that can too easily help us cover mistakes that should be exposed.

I noted the difference between godly sorrow and worldly sorrow earlier. David is a perfect example of godly sorrow. Once he finally realized his error, he genuinely repented. He didn't try to justify himself or blame others. Instead, he turned to God in humility and faith. He feared God more than he feared the consequences of his actions or the public shame he would experience. That fear led him to repentance.

The king who preceded David, a man named Saul, is an example of the opposite type of sorrow. In 1 Samuel 15, we read about King Saul receiving a command from God to attack and completely destroy a people group called the Amalekites. Saul and his men partially carried out the order, but they spared the king and kept the best of the livestock they captured for themselves. To top it off, Saul set up a monument to himself, as if he were a mighty king to be feared.

The next day, the prophet Samuel approached Saul about his rebellion, and Saul tried to justify his actions by saying that they spared the best animals as a sacrifice to God. Samuel wasn't buying Saul's excuses though. He called Saul out for being arrogant and rebellious, and he told him that God was going to strip the kingdom of Israel away from him.

Saul was alarmed by Samuel's words and acknowledged that he was wrong. But his response showed that his real concern wasn't pleasing God but saving face with the people.

He pleaded with Samuel, "I have sinned. But please honor me before the elders of my people and before Israel" (v. 30).

What a difference from David's repentant prayer to God: "Against you, and you alone, have I sinned" (Ps. 51:4 NLT). David wanted his relationship with God to be made right. Saul wanted to keep his position before the people.

Worldly sorrow focuses on us. Godly sorrow focuses on God.

I've said it over and over: you *will* have regret in your life, but what's important is how you respond to it. If we're going to be a generation that overcomes regret, we need to respond with godly sorrow. Worldly sorrow leads to bondage, slavery, and death. Godly sorrow leads to salvation, deliverance, and life.

Before we move on, notice how David was finally brought to repentance. He allowed someone to speak into his life. I'm sure David's conscience had been bothering him, but that wasn't enough. He needed to be confronted by someone who knew him, knew the situation, and wanted the best for him.

Sometimes God confronts us directly and personally. Other times, God uses people close to us to speak into our lives.

Be open to the awakening that comes through other people. One of the great benefits of walking through life with others is the accountability our intimacy and fellowship create. We should allow those who know us well and believe in our future to speak into our lives.

If you don't have a Nathan to keep you accountable, you could be walking down a treacherous path alone. Let trusted, wise people speak into your life. Invite them to point out your errors. It's far better to listen to counsel than to compound mistakes and continue to hurt those around you.

Awakened to Consequences

One reason we try to bury our mistakes is because we don't want to face the consequences. Again, it's that misguided self-defense mechanism. But things that are buried have a way of coming back to haunt us. (That's the story line of most old horror movies, right?) If we want to move past regret, we must face the consequences of our actions.

Remember, regret changes our future not by taking our problems away but by teaching us and changing us through our problems. In other words, the way *out* is *through*. And that means accepting the natural consequences of our mistakes.

When David confessed his sin, Nathan assured him that God had taken away his sin but also warned him he would still suffer consequences (2 Sam. 12:14). For David, the consequence was the death of the newborn baby with Bathsheba and ongoing violence in his own family.

It's important to understand the difference between punishment and consequences. We should not assume God was punishing David for his behavior. Why? Because the punishment he deserved was far greater. God didn't make David pay for his sins. Instead, he showed David mercy and grace—but he still allowed him to experience the effect of his poor choices.

David didn't become the mighty king of Israel who we know as the "man after God's own heart" because God let him off the hook and shielded him from the consequences of his actions. He gained that title by leaning into God even through his regret and despair.

The same dynamic probably played out for all of us when our parents or teachers allowed us to experience certain consequences for our actions. At the time, it probably felt like punishment, but we were not paying for our mistakes—we were being encouraged to learn from them. If the lesson sunk in, we allowed the discomfort to motivate us to change, and we grew through the process.

David clearly understood this. When he learned his son would die, he pleaded with God for a different outcome. He fasted, prayed, and slept on the ground for days. But when he heard his son was dead, he got up, washed himself, went to the house of the Lord, and worshiped.

His servants were confused. They asked, "Why are you acting like this?" David replied that while his son was alive, he could pray and ask God for mercy. But now that his son was dead, all he could do was move forward. So before he broke his fast and ate, he worshiped God.[1]

What does this mean for us? God does not deal with us according to our sins but according to his mercy. When we are dealing with the messes we've made, we can trust that God is actually helping us minimize the consequences and pain of our wrong actions. But at the same time, we must maintain a humble, worshipful attitude, recognizing both the seriousness of our errors and the sovereignty of God.

Awakened to Grace

I already mentioned that God showed David grace by limiting the consequences of his actions. I could also say that the consequences themselves were a demonstration of grace, because God was teaching David to think and act differently.

No matter what happens, we can see God's grace at work

in our mess. God doesn't leave us trapped in pain or cut off from blessings—he sets us free. He covers a multitude of sins and, if we let him, propels us further than we could ever go on our own.

The enemy would love for us to think that our future has been ruined by the mistakes of our pasts. The Bible says in Jesus we are a new creation (2 Cor. 5:17), and there is no longer any condemnation for those who are in him (Rom. 8:1). That means that our regret can point us to grace, and our mistakes become a testimony to God's mercy and redemption.

David knew that no matter what he walked through, whether external attacks or personal failures, God was always on his side. Throughout the book of Psalms, we see him crying out to God with his questions and heartaches. But in each of his psalms, David finishes his prayer by thanking God and affirming his faith in him. We are recipients of the same grace, and we must live with the same faith and gratitude, even when the circumstances and consequences seem less than ideal.

Awakened to Our Worth

David understood that his relationship with God was based on grace and mercy and not on his actions. That is the message of the cross as well. We don't draw near to God on our own merit but through faith in Jesus.

In order to respond properly to regret, we must know that our worth goes beyond behavior and, instead, is rooted in our relationship to God.

If we tie worth to performance, we are setting ourselves

up for failure. Maybe not at first, because we can usually live for a while without making any major mistakes. But sooner or later, we are going to fail. And if our sense of worth is dependent on our behavior, the shame of failure will pull us to the ground and hold us there.

Our worth is based on two facts. First, we are made in God's image. And second, we can identify ourselves with Jesus and receive new life in him. The life we now live, we live in Jesus. That means that even when we are less than perfect, his perfection is still ours. Even when we show our flaws, his identity is still what counts.

Again, this does not give us license to fail or an excuse to sin. But it does give us reason to rise again when we inevitably do both. Our value in God's eyes is as unchanging as his love for us, because we have been forgiven, chosen, and accepted by Jesus.

When I came back on staff after that year of self-reflection, the temptation to operate in insecurity was real. I couldn't deny my past mistakes and immaturities, and I could have allowed those things to define my view of myself going forward. I could have allowed my past mistakes to strip me of my worth or force me to try to prove my value.

But I chose not to. It wasn't easy, but I turned my focus to the grace that I've received through Jesus instead of the shame of my own actions. I focused on my calling in Jesus, not my skill set or leadership abilities. And I depended on my his work through me, not my works or my efforts.

The hidden benefit of regret is that it reminds us of our deficiencies and insufficiencies, and that propels us to find our value in Jesus alone.

Awakened to Growth

I once heard someone say that you find out who you really are on a golf course. I believe it. I've seen people break their clubs, throw them in the water, and walk off the course steaming mad. Others habitually look for something to blame for errant shots: that car that honked five streets over or a bird singing up in a tree.

If you've ever played golf, you know things don't always go the way you want them to. Temper tantrums and petty excuses are par for the course, if you'll excuse the pun. But no matter how many lost balls, sand traps, or weeds get in the way of a good shot, the best golfers never lose their drive for the game. Instead, they strive to *improve* their game.

To improve, of course, they have to focus on their game. They have to address the variables within their control, not the variables beyond that control. So they work on their form, practice their putts, experiment with different clubs, and build their skills.

In the same way, we can learn from the mistakes we make on the playing course of life. But that will only happen if we control our emotions, avoid blaming everyone else, and focus on growth.

It is remarkably liberating to say, "I was wrong, and I'm ready to accept the responsibility." The second you do that, shame loses its power. You have nothing to hide, so all your emotional and mental energy can be focused on what needs to be done to grow, change, and succeed.

David seems to have grown through his experience with Uriah and Bathsheba. Psalm 51 demonstrates authentic humility and a deep commitment to God. His reaction to

Nathan was heartfelt and genuine, and most tellingly, we don't see him continuing on with this lifestyle. He never again commits adultery or orchestrates someone's murder. Instead, we see a life of godly fear and a life committed to God's work and following his will. David used his regret to focus on the weaknesses that his errors revealed, and it created a platform for many more years of leadership and influence. Despite David's very serious sins, the biblical testimony of his life is overwhelmingly positive.

That is the power of grace: it not only forgives but also transforms. When you draw close to God and experience his grace, you will be motivated and empowered to grow.

Awakened to Our Future

Let's go back to the golf course for a minute. One thing I've always loved is how golf challenges its players to be mentally strong. In that sense, golf can teach us a lot about how to deal with regrets.

My father often reminded me when I was growing up that 99 percent of golf is played in your head, not on the course. When you're playing at your best, it seems as if you're unstoppable. But if you hit one bad shot, it can change your mental game in a second. If you start losing the game in your mind, you'll lose your cool and make more and more mistakes. One errant shot can ruin the entire hole and sometimes the entire round.

Professional golfer Tiger Woods once said that after a shot, he allows himself ten steps to react. Within those ten steps, he can get as mad at himself as he wants. He can overthink his last shot repeatedly. But once he's taken those ten steps, he has to move on and focus on his next shot. He knows there's nothing he can do about the past stroke, and focusing instead on strategizing his next shot gives him the greatest chance of saving the hole and making par.[2]

Just like in golf, the best way to overcome mistakes is to acknowledge them, process our regret for a time, and then focus on what we need to do next. That's the progression we looked at earlier in 2 Corinthians 7:11.

Mistake → Remorse → Repentance → Victory

Of course, that doesn't mean we should flippantly forget the seriousness of past errors, but it does mean we should avoid dwelling on them to the point that they hold us back and affect the rest of our life.

It's time for our generation to change its narrative.

The Hebrew word for regret is *atsab*. The first meaning of that term is "hurt, pain, grief, torture," but the second meaning is "to fashion, form, or stretch into shape."[3] The world knows regret by the first meaning: a torturous pain that grieves our future. But as sons and daughters of God, we can reshape regret to be a tool that will fashion, form, and stretch us into a new shape.

I truly believe we're going to be a generation that changes how the world sees things, just as David did. Following his example, we must face our faults and regrets, move past what *could have been*, and look toward what *can be*!

As sons and daughters of God, we are called to bring change in this world. To bring light from darkness, to bring hope in hopelessness, and to bring life from death. We are called to flip the script on our past mistakes. Rather than allowing regret to become an anchor in our life, we can use it to propel us forward.

The last chapter of your life has not been written yet. What matters most is not what has happened to you but what you are going to do about it.

WE ARE AN **AWAKENED** GENERATION,

NOT A REGRETFUL GENERATION.

OUR MISTAKES POINT US TO GRACE.

OUR REMORSE MOTIVATES US TO GROW.

AND IN HUMILITY AND WISDOM

WE BUILD OUR FUTURE IN GOD.

We should be too big to take offense and too noble to give it.

Abraham Lincoln

AS BELIEVERS IN CHRIST, we are called to be unified. One church. One body. The enemy knows this, and he'll do everything he can to tear us apart. One of his most effective tactics is holding a grudge. When a grudge, or offense, is built up against someone else, it's one of the hardest things to tear down.

An offended friend is harder to win back than a fortified city. Arguments separate friends like a gate locked with bars. (Prov. 18:19 NLT)

You might have been taught as a child to forgive others and let go of grudges. These tasks are much simpler to say than to do. That is, it's easier to say "I forgive you" than to actually forgive someone. It's easier to just sweep hurts under the rug, act like nothing happened, and pretend like you're okay.

When I was younger, my parents would make my brothers and me stop and hug whenever we fought. It was their way of reminding us that we still loved each other, despite our anger. Although we were upset over whatever had happened in the moment, a hug made us hit pause on our conflict. It gave us a chance to regain our composure and talk things through. As a result, we were less likely to harbor anger toward each other. It's like we released our anger in the hug. I fully realize how cheesy that sounds—but hey, it worked!

I love the fact that my family has always fought for our relationships. We're not perfect, by any means, but we've learned to fight *for* rather than *against* each other. My parents always told us to "Have the hard conversations with your brothers. Although there may be tears and pain, keep fighting for the relationship. Don't pull away as soon as things get difficult." My parents understood that if we held on to grudges, it would tear our family apart.

In the same way that the Beveres are a family, all of us are brothers and sisters in Christ. We are one big family, which means that we need to start fighting for unity.

Our generation is far too quick to get offended and far too slow to forgive. We're also really good at burying our pain and really bad at having honest conversations in order to work through it. God wants to show us how to live differently, how to have those hard conversations, how to fight for unity, and how to value relationships.

The Bible gives us multiple examples of people being offended and needing forgiveness. As a matter of fact, many of the greatest Bible heroes had to choose to forgive others—including Jesus as he hung on the cross. I'd like to look at two biblical heroes in particular: Joseph and David.

Before I jump into these two stories, though, let me share one of my own.

UNCOVERING MY OFFENDED HEART

I never thought I would deal with offense, to be honest. I mean, my dad literally wrote the book on it! And not only did he write the book, he personally taught my brothers and me principles that would keep us from holding on to offenses. If anybody knew how dangerous grudges are—and why we should stay as far away from them as possible—it was us!

But one December a few years ago, I heard that a female friend of mine was spreading rumors about me that were nowhere close to the truth. I couldn't believe this was happening to me. I was working *extremely* hard to be a man of integrity and purity, and the rumors were undermining that with surprising effectiveness.

I'm not a guy who shies away from confrontation, so I did what the Bible says. I went directly to the girl and talked about it. I discovered I had unintentionally done something to hurt her, and her comments about me were coming out of anger and hurt feelings. I sincerely apologized, cleared it up, and thought that was the end of it.

It wasn't. Even though the original conflict was resolved, the rumors were still making the rounds. And I found out a virtual stranger was making it clear she believed the rumors. When I talked with this girl, she started the conversation by saying, "People just really don't like you." Ouch! She added that other mutual acquaintances were saying I wasn't a good person either.

Frustrated by it all, I kept fighting for my reputation. Time after time, I thought I had things cleared up, but then I would hear more gossip and negativity.

This is the part of the story where the offense in my heart started to really show itself. I learned that, even after all the conversations, this person truly believed the bad things she had heard about me. So I did my best to distance myself from her and ignore her. But I was overly sensitive to her reactions whenever I did have to talk to her.

Her response to me was less than positive as well. Looking back, I probably deserved that. I wasn't treating her or leading her in a humble, healthy way. Yes, I felt like my name had been slandered, but I was acting like she was the problem, and she didn't deserve that.

Unfortunately, it gets worse. I won't go into the details, but soon a romance began developing between one of my friends and this particular girl. Suddenly I felt betrayed by that friend as well. As a result, I tried whatever I could to hinder their relationship. But my attempts to win my friend's loyalty only succeeded in getting me excluded from the group.

I felt like a total victim (which is a typical sign of offense, by the way). In my mind all I was trying to do was stand up for myself, and what I got in return was more hardship. I tried taking the matter to others, but it seemed like more and more people were taking sides against me. When I did find a few people who took my side, their sympathy only fueled my frustration.

I felt so alone. I thought everyone was out to get me. My leadership abilities were affected. I became harsher and developed a short temper with my team. Those who were close to me knew that I wasn't myself. But when they tried to speak wisdom into the situation, I refused to listen.

Five months into this drama, some of my friends staged an intervention. The situation was beyond toxic, and it needed to end. They sat down with me and the couple, and we all had an amazing conversation. Tears were shed and true hearts were exposed. We all acknowledged our hurt and decided to forgive each other.

I felt a lot better initially. But when the couple continued to make their relationship more official, something ugly stirred inside of me. I was cordial with both of them but never genuinely nice. And I went back to recruiting people to my side of "the battle."

This went on for three more months. Then one day I was talking about the situation with my fiancée. I was rehearsing all the reasons I had to be upset and complaining that these two people had turned me into a villain.

As I finished my sob story, a light bulb turned on in my heart. I realized I was offended. I had said "I forgive you" to this couple, but I wasn't sure I truly meant it. I wondered, *If Jesus were physically present with me, would he say that I have genuinely forgiven them? Am I treating them in a way that reflects his heart of forgiveness?* The answer was a resounding no, and it made my heart extremely sad.

I immediately went to my friend and apologized. I said, "I'm so sad and sorry. I can't believe I've been so blind. I don't care who's right. I just want to let go of this offense. I am for you. I'm not against you. Please forgive me!"

I felt like something was lifted off my shoulders. The next day, I left for a trip to South Africa. I was given an unexpected opportunity to speak for Hillsong South Africa, and I felt such power and authority in the message I delivered there. I believe I was able to speak so freely because I was no longer carrying the weight of my offense. Without that burden, there was abundant room in my life for God's blessings.

Later, I had a good conversation with the girl I had been offended by as well. We both apologized and acknowledged false ideas we had believed about each other. All grudges were released, and the relationship was finally truly restored.

As I let go of the offense, I watched as amazing gifts came into my life. Speaking at Hillsong was only the beginning. Within the next month, I was offered my first book contract—for this book. I purchased my first home at just twenty-four. More importantly, I married the woman of my dreams! I thank God that I didn't enter into marriage with offense in my heart, because this union has been the greatest gift in my life.

I share that story because it illustrates the subtle yet incredibly powerful nature of offense. It didn't really matter who did what to whom at the beginning—the issue was that I was unable to let go of the offense. Not only that, but I couldn't even see that I was offended, because my offense had blinded me.

THE POWER OF FORGIVENESS

If offense is powerful, forgiveness is even more powerful. God can use the offenses we face to teach us the beautiful yet difficult power of forgiveness. As we release the things we've held on to, we open the door for God to shower us with his incredible goodness and blessing.

The word I want to speak over our generation is this: *blessed*.

Once I allowed forgiveness to overpower offense, blessings followed. That's what God does, because he delights in unity.

Look what David wrote in Psalm 133:1–3.

> How good and pleasant it is
>> when God's people live together in unity!
>
> It is like precious oil poured on the head,
>> running down on the beard,
> running down on Aaron's beard,
>> down on the collar of his robe.
> It is as if the dew of Hermon
>> were falling on Mount Zion.
> For there the LORD bestows his blessing,
>> even life forevermore.

Notice the way he describes the blessings that follow a decision to be unified. I'm not saying that when you forgive someone who has offended you, unending blessings will immediately flow into your life. But the connection is clear, and God is true to his promises. When you and I choose to live in forgiveness rather than offense, God's blessings are free to flow through us.

Our generation can be quick to judge and get offended. But if we want to experience the fullness of God's blessings and the fulfillment of his promises, we have to be the first to step forward and forgive. We must make the first move!

God sets the example in taking initiative to restore broken relationships. The apostle Paul wrote: "But God demonstrates his own love for us in this: While we were still sinners, Christ died for us" (Rom. 5:8).

In other words, when we were totally undeserving of forgiveness, Jesus gave up his life for us. He died for all sins, over all time. He didn't put them on a scale to see how bad they were. He didn't pick and choose. He didn't judge what was fair to forgive and what wasn't. No, he simply gave up his life on a cross to offer forgiveness for *all* of our sins.

Before we can forgive, we must recognize that we are a forgiven people. Despite all the terrible things we've thought, done, or said, God loves us and loves to forgive us.

When we show that attitude toward people who have hurt, betrayed, or offended us, we will stand out and be noticed as a generation that is different than any other. We will open ourselves up to receiving blessing, and we will become a blessing to those around us as well.

There is no clearer example of the blessings that come through forgiveness than Joseph. His is a story of jealousy, hatred, violence, betrayal—and the overwhelming power of grace.

JOSEPH: BLESSING IN FORGIVENESS

Joseph was one of the youngest sons of a man named Jacob. His story begins in Genesis 37. The Bible doesn't hide the fact that Joseph was Jacob's favorite son, and everyone—including his brothers—knew it. If you have a lot of siblings like I do, you know this was a problem!

To make matters worse, Joseph had two dreams about his brothers bowing down to him, and *he told them about those dreams.* As much as I like having healthy competition with my brothers, even I would be smart enough to keep things like that to myself!

Eventually the favoritism and the dreams were more than Joseph's brothers could handle, and they allowed their insane jealousy of him to take control. They kidnapped him, sold him into slavery, and mocked his arrogant dreams.

If there was ever a time when a person deserved to be offended, Joseph earned that right. Can you imagine the people you trusted most growing up turning on you and selling you into slavery? Your life is *over* all because you had some swagger and confidence, with a little family dysfunction thrown in.

Joseph was taken to Egypt, where he was sold to a ruler named Potiphar. Joseph served Potiphar faithfully for eleven years. God's grace and wisdom shined clearly through Joseph, and as a result, Potiphar made Joseph the overseer of his house. Joseph made the most of a grim situation.

But just as things were looking up, everything fell apart. Potiphar's wife made a move on Joseph and tried to convince him to sleep with her. But he refused. In fact, he ran out of the house. Before he could pull away, though, she ripped off a piece of his clothing, yelled for her servants, and accused Joseph of trying to rape her.

As a result, Joseph was sentenced to prison. He was basically back in the same place he found himself when his brothers sold him into slavery. It would make complete sense for him to be bitter about all the wrong that had been done to him. He had to be wondering, *Why? What did I do to deserve this? I was more faithful to Potiphar than his own wife! I served my master, and* this *is my reward? Why didn't my brothers just kill me? That would have been easier!*

If you already know the end of the story, it's easy to take Joseph's ups and downs lightly. But sitting in that jail cell, do you think it ever crossed Joseph's mind that God could be using his hardship for good? I think most of us would be overwhelmed with thoughts of revenge. We'd be out for blood!

Joseph eventually got out of prison, and in a crazy turn of events, he was elevated to second-in-command over all of Egypt. If you aren't familiar with the story, it's worth reading. First, he interpreted a wild dream the Pharaoh had, winning the ruler's favor. Then, because the dream foretold a famine, he was put in charge of storing up food before the famine came. Seven years later, just as he predicted, famine hit all the nations in that region. Because of Joseph's preparations, Egypt was the only land with food.

Because the famine struck more than just Egypt, Joseph's brothers eventually came looking for help. When they stood before Joseph, they didn't recognize their own brother. But he knew who they were. Joseph had the power to kill them or lock them up forever. The tables had finally turned, and the control was on Joseph's side.

At first, Joseph hid his identity, because he wanted to make sure his brothers truly changed. He even created a couple of tests to see if they would remain loyal to each other, which they passed.

Eventually he revealed himself to his family. They were understandably terrified of retribution, but he assured them that he would not harm them. Somehow he had the capacity to forgive them.

Think about that. On a human level, his brothers were completely to blame for the painful aspects of Joseph's past.

But Joseph saw beyond that. He recognized God's hand at work, and he was able to forgive his brothers by acknowledging God's greater plan.

Then he shares this profound truth with his brothers: "It was not you who sent me here, but God" (Gen. 45:8).

When you go through hardships, it's easy to feel like someone else put you there. But you're not there because of someone else. You're there because God allowed you to be.

When Joseph was sold into slavery, do you think God looked at Jesus and said, "I'm stumped over here. What are we going to do?" Of course not! God knew what was going to happen, and he knew he was going to use it for Joseph's benefit and for Israel's salvation. Through Joseph, his entire family was saved, and so was the nation of Egypt.

No matter how bad or hopeless things look, God can use your circumstances to elevate you and serve others. It's up to you, though, to determine how you'll respond to difficulties.

If you're in the middle of a trial related to some offense, and you're holding on to that offense, you may feel certain that God isn't there for you and that he won't bring you a miracle. Well, you're probably right. He likely won't change your circumstances until you learn to forgive. Holding on to a grudge can keep you out of the will of God, and it's no one's fault but your own.

If you hold on to an offense, God may withhold miracles and blessing for your own protection. There are two reasons for that.

First, he knows you are likely to use any power you have to hurt the people who hurt you. Therefore, he won't give you very much power. You'll likely find your influence and authority limited, because you need to mature before you are given more power. I suspect God would have left Joseph in prison if he had insisted on holding on to his anger toward his brothers. Why? Because had he not forgiven them, the power he received from Pharaoh would have only amplified his hatred and even allowed him to kill them.

Second, God may not open as many doors of opportunity or pour out as many blessings on you because you might use them for yourself. If you are operating from a place of hurt, then you are likely struggling with insecurity and selfishness as well. Being offended makes you feel like a victim, which makes you more likely to use anything and everything you gain in life to prop up your fractured ego. I'm sure Joseph did some deep soul-searching in that prison. He had to face his anger, his trauma, his fear. He was able to process those things, turn to God, and genuinely forgive. And that's when all of heaven started working in his favor.

You may be thinking, "But Arden, you don't know what they did to me!" I hear you, but I'd counter by saying that you don't know what you do to God by holding on to anger and refusing to forgive his people. My father makes this amazing statement in his book *The Bait of Satan*: "A person who cannot forgive has forgotten how great a debt God has forgiven them."[1]

The question is, do we truly understand what God did for us? He sent his Son to save us as the ultimate demonstration of forgiveness, despite everything we've done against him. What right do we have to hold resentment toward someone else?

To forgive is one of the greatest, yet most difficult, things we can do in life. Yet it is the doorway to the greatest blessings.

Joseph set the example for our generation. Rather than holding on to bitterness or seeking revenge against those who have offended us, it's time to trust God's sovereignty. He has a plan. He knows what he's doing. And if we can align ourselves with his grace—the same grace he showed us—we will be a catalyst for good everywhere we go. We will change our trajectory and that of those around us through the power and blessing of forgiveness.

SAUL AND DAVID: BLESSING IN SUBMISSION

It is especially difficult (but especially important) to know how to correctly process negative emotions stirred up by offensive behavior when the person we need to forgive is someone we expected more from in the first place.

We all have leaders we look up to in our lives such as parents, teachers, bosses, pastors, government officials. It's hard enough to navigate the forgiveness process with peers. But how do we forgive when someone in authority does us wrong?

David looked up to King Saul as a father figure, and Saul welcomed David into his army after his epic victory over Goliath. Saul's son, Jonathan, quickly became David's best friend. Things seemed to be looking pretty good for David. Eventually, the king even offered David his daughter's hand in marriage, and David became his son-in-law.

In 1 Samuel 18, however, we read that Saul noticed the people admired David more than him. He went nearly insane with envy, and he began plotting ways to get David killed. In an instant, David went from a son and friend of the family to an enemy to be hunted and killed.

Think about this from David's perspective. You look up to Saul because he was anointed by God to rule the kingdom.

You've served him faithfully. You've fought his battles and won his wars. And not only is he your king, he's also your father-in-law. And after all that, he wants you *dead*!

I've seen some rough relationships between in-laws, but nothing quite like this!

David had every right to be offended. Saul was jealous of David's popularity and wanted to take his life because of it. It didn't seem to matter that David had never wronged him and had, instead, always served him. To complicate things even more, David knew that God had anointed him to become the next king of Israel (1 Sam. 16:12–13). So Saul was not only trying to take his life but he was also trying to rob God's chosen people of their next anointed king. David should have been able to hold at least a little bit of a grudge, wouldn't you think? Maybe he could give in to self-righteous anger and take a shot at the king? It would just be self-defense, right?

But that's not how David thought, and that's not how he lived.

Instead of fighting back, David and his men ran for their lives into the wilderness. Saul and his men chased after them. A few chapters later, in a scene laced with drama, Saul entered a cave where David and his men were hiding. Saul didn't have a clue that David was there. In the darkness of the cave, David sneaked up to Saul and cut off a small piece of his clothing. As Saul and his men were about to ride off, David held up the fabric from Saul's cloak and yelled out, "See what I have! I could have killed you, but I didn't!" With this realization, Saul gave up the chase and told his men to go home.[2]

The peace treaty didn't last long though. Before too much time had passed, Saul's anger flared up again, and he gathered his army to hunt down his enemy, David. One night,

God put Saul's men into a deep sleep. David and his men snuck into Saul's camp and eventually made their way to Saul's tent. David was one command away from having one of his men kill Saul in his sleep. But he didn't: instead, he made this profound statement: "Who can lay a hand on the LORD's anointed and be guiltless?" (1 Sam. 26:9).

The lesson we can glean from this moment is that no matter how mistreated we feel, and no matter how much of a right we might have to retaliate, it's not our place to take revenge, *especially* against a leader in our lives. We must leave the offense with God and allow him to bring justice into an unfair situation.

I realize this is much easier said than done, and I say this from personal experience. I remember a difficulty I once had with a former boss. I felt like his behavior in the situation didn't reflect godly values, so I talked to my dad about it. He said, "Son, just because all authority is *from* God doesn't mean all authority is *godly*." In other words, God gives leaders authority, but that doesn't mean everything they do is perfect or sanctioned by him. Like David, we need to be able to separate an authority's actions from their position. We can honor their position without approving of everything they do.

Let me clarify here that when I say "honor their position," I'm *not* talking about excusing obvious moral failure, abusive situations, or illegal conduct. If a leader's behavior is clearly harmful—whether in the workplace, the church, volunteer settings, or within the family—the people under their oversight will likely need to respond in some way. That reaction will depend on the specific situation.

Many times, though, the issue is not moral or criminal but personal. Maybe it's mistreatment or injustice, whether real or perceived. Maybe it's a character flaw in the leader. Maybe it's a decision we don't agree with. Maybe it's being criticized unfairly or spoken to harshly or being ignored or shut down. Maybe it's a personality conflict.

Whether we agree with our leaders or not, we can still honor the position they hold. We can still obey them. Obviously this doesn't mean that we obey them if they ask us to sin, but it does mean that we see them as the Lord's positioned authority. Leaders are not perfect, but that doesn't mean we have the right to respond poorly to their imperfections.

We have to understand that the kingdom of God isn't a democracy. It's a theocracy, meaning God alone is in charge. In many decisions, therefore, he doesn't ask our opinion and he doesn't give us a vote. He simply asks us to submit to him and the authorities he has placed in our lives. So when someone is in a place of authority, it's not *our* place to judge him or her. It's God's! Our job is to continually honor the position of authority, even if the behavior isn't godly or we feel mistreated.

If we look back at our story, we'll see that David stayed true to his principles, and God honored his decision to submit to authority. David continued to love Saul and be faithful and unoffended by him, despite all of Saul's wrongdoings. He recognized and respected the authority given by God.

The conflict didn't last forever. Eventually, Saul died. Even after all the former king had done to make his life miserable, David still tore his clothes and mourned for Saul's death. Then God gave David the throne (2 Sam. 1–2).

What would have happened if David had taken the throne by force? If he had started a civil war or assassinated Saul? While we can't know for sure, I'm convinced the end of

David's story would have been much different. He would have short-circuited God's process and ignored God's decisions, and that never ends well.

Instead of taking matters into his own hands, he trusted God's call and timing. He suffered for a while, but in his suffering, he also grew. He matured into a tested leader and a person of integrity, who could be trusted by God and people. And when the day came, David was able to step into his future with a clean conscience and divine blessing.

Submitting to and honoring authorities opens our lives to divine blessing. It's a demonstration of trust, not just in human leadership, but in God's leadership. And God will honor that trust by building our character and our influence.

Our generation is called to leadership and influence, but in order to fulfill that calling, we need to overcome hurt and step into God's favor and blessing. Like Joseph, we must overcome the ways we are offended with forgiveness. And like David, we must honor and respect those in authority, even when we see their imperfections.

As we turn offense into forgiveness, God will mature us, elevate us, and carry us to victory. We will step into the calling that is upon our generation: to be blessed and to be a blessing, in whatever we do.

WE ARE A **BLESSED** GENERATION,

NOT AN OFFENDED GENERATION.

WE KNOW HOW TO FORGIVE AND SHOW GRACE,

HOW TO LOVE UNCONDITIONALLY

AND SHOW MERCY ALWAYS.

SEVEN

LACKING

When the Lord makes it clear you're to follow him in this new direction, focus fully on him and refuse to be distracted by comparisons with others.

Charles Swindoll

WE LIVE IN A CULTURE of comparison. We're constantly seeing the highlight reels of other people's lives—perfect posts, funny captions, and creative videos—and it's become second nature for us to compare our lives to those perfect images. As a result, we often begin to wonder why our own lives aren't as great as everyone else's.

It can leave us feeling like life is a race we're running against everyone else. A race to get the most followers, the best jobs, the coolest friends. Why is that? Because comparison leads to competition.

But here's the problem. Life isn't supposed to be a competition. It's supposed to be a journey. Your walk will never look exactly like someone else's. We all have a unique, God-designed path to follow. And if our gaze is fixed on people around us rather than the path we're on, we'll find ourselves pouring all we have into a race with no finish line.

When you're racing, all you can see is who's around you. You look to the right and the left to see if you're winning, to see how far ahead or behind you are compared to everyone else.

But when you approach life as a journey, you focus on where you are, where you're going, and what you experience along the way.

As a generation, we need to change the way we view life. The trap of the comparison race leaves us feeling inadequate, deficient, and lacking, but the freedom of enjoying the journey opens us up to the beauty all around us.

STOP LOOKING AT WHAT'S LACKING

The problem with comparison, of course, is that it never ends. There's always someone better, bigger, faster, taller, smarter. So if we base our self-worth or our hope for the future on how well we measure up against other people, we're only setting ourselves up for a struggle with inferiority. The result of a life based on comparison is a nagging sense of lack.

Our generation seems fixated on comparison, so it's no wonder we deal with feelings of inferiority, of inadequacy, of lack. We don't value who we are or see what we're capable of because we're too distracted evaluating ourselves against those around us. It's hard to have energy to believe in your future when you are overwhelmed just fending off fears that you don't measure up.

If you grew up with expectations about your future but secretly felt like you couldn't fulfill them (or didn't even want to fulfill them), then you know the debilitating feeling of not measuring up. It's not uncommon for kids to grow up under the expectations of others. Some parents expect their children to take on the family business, while others push their children to have a better life than they did.

I know what that's like. I grew up with parents who are famous authors and speakers. They have spent years traveling the world to share what God placed on their hearts, and they have made an incredible impact along the way. Many times I have felt the weight of expectation that comes with our family legacy. Like many pastors' kids, there was a subtle expectation (or, at least, a *perceived* expectation) that my brothers and I would one day work in the family ministry. Whether that expectation came from people in the church or me, the pressure was always there. And the impact of my family's ministry wasn't just in a local church but on a global scale. So in my mind, if I failed to meet this expectation, I'd be letting thousands of people down around the world.

People would ask me all the time, "Are you going to be the next John Bevere?" Imagine how that felt! Even worse, I didn't have a desire to go into the family business. Growing up, I didn't feel like I had the calling that the rest of my family had. As a result, I felt a strong, pervading sense of lack, like I was failing as a son to my parents and failing as a son of God.

That feeling of lack caused me to question everything that was unique about me. I wondered how I would ever be able to live up to my father's legacy. Thoughts of fear and failure tormented me. *Even if I do follow in my parents' footsteps, could I even begin to fill their shoes? If I don't become one of the great Beveres, will that mean I am inadequate? Will my family and others think I am a failure?*

The feeling of inadequacy only made things worse. I began to live with deep feelings of inferiority. I developed a stutter, and I mumbled when I spoke. I lost confidence that what I said mattered.

When we constantly compare ourselves to others, we lose confidence in who we are. Comparison causes us to forget or despise the special things God has placed in us. So we draw back. We dismiss the dreams he's given us because we don't think we have what it takes to accomplish them. We feel inadequate. It becomes natural for us to shine a spotlight on the things we believe we're missing rather than the things we do well.

For example, if you were to see a line of bushes with one bush missing, the missing bush would stick out in your mind. You wouldn't recognize all the other bushes, because you'd be focusing on the one that was not there. The same is true for our lives. When we have a feeling of lack, we lose focus of what we do have and concentrate on what we don't have.

When I lost my ability to speak well because of my stutter, I could only focus on that. I lost sight of what I *could* do and only focused on what I *couldn't* do.

Comparison doesn't just focus our attention on our limitations, it also focuses our attention on what we can't change. Rather than seeing what we *can* improve, we see the things we *can't* improve.

Think about what you see when you look in the mirror. For most of us, it's easy to pick out the features we don't like and more difficult to find the ones we do. We think things like, *If only I had better teeth . . . If only I had nicer hair . . . If only I were taller . . . If only I were thinner . . .*

Here's the thing though. God is not the one focused on our lack—we are. It doesn't hold him back, but it can certainly hold us back if we let it.

God isn't disappointed in us.

God isn't setting us up for failure.

God isn't pointing out our weaknesses.

God isn't comparing us to those around us.

God isn't holding us to impossible expectations.

We notice most what we think is lacking, but God only notices who he made us to be. God made us in his image, and he is happy with the result. He is proud of who we are. Our generation struggles with a feeling of lack, of falling short, of failing to meet expectations, but that is not God's view of us at all.

The word God speaks over us is not *lacking*; it's *complete*.

That completeness comes from him, in him, and through him. We do have areas of lack, for sure. It would be silly and dishonest to deny it. But our lack does not define us; God defines us. His completeness is our completeness. His sufficiency is our sufficiency. His wholeness is our wholeness.

HOW GOD VIEWS HIS CREATION

I'd like to highlight five truths about us in our relationship with God that help us overcome the feelings of lack, inferiority, and insufficiency that so easily assail our minds.

We Are Completed by God

When we make a list of everything we dislike about ourselves, we're actually nitpicking God's handiwork because we are all his masterpieces. He created us with no second guesses, no regrets, and no mistakes. He created us the way we are for a reason! God created us in his image, and *nothing* is lacking in his creation.

When it came to my future and the angst I experienced at being compared to my parents, I completely mishandled those expectations. I didn't see my potential and calling through God's eyes. Rather, I looked at all the things I didn't have and all the things I couldn't do. I focused on what was lacking and refused to own the skills and abilities God had placed in my life. In turn, I stopped becoming the person he created me to be.

The revelation that changed me was not a revelation of my greatness but a revelation of my completeness in God's eyes. Once I realized that he made me who I am and was happy with the result, everything changed.

We're not great because of our own potential and ability. We're great because of God! If we focus on our imperfections and limitations, we're essentially insulting him.

For so much of my life, I was unsure of who I was because I was too caught up in comparing myself to others. It wasn't until I stopped measuring myself by everyone else's merits and truly relied on God that I was able to find complete wholeness in him.

I know that I am who I am today because of the call my heavenly Father placed on me and the way that my earthly father led me. Ministry has always been a part of me, even though I tried to run from it when I was growing up. My dad is—and always will be—my inspiration and my hero. But I'm not going to be the next John Paul Bevere. I will be Arden Christopher Bevere instead. I have to be myself, not my dad or anyone else. I've learned that when I stop comparing myself to other ministry leaders and instead focus on what God says about me and has called me to do, I am complete.

As individuals, as leaders, and as a generation, we are complete in God and accepted by God. That is our starting place. From there, we can grow and improve, and we can become who we are called to be. But we don't have to do anything special before we are accepted, and we don't have to add something to our lives or fix something that is broken before we are complete. We begin from a place of completeness.

We Are Made Whole by God

When we feel like we are lacking in some crucial way, we can turn to God and find grace in our weakness.

Of all the Bible stories I heard growing up, there is one that I always related to in a special way. The story of Joshua is an account that deeply encouraged me when I felt lacking and inadequate.

We first encounter the strong military leader after he had been called by Moses to lead an army to attack the Amalekites (Exod. 17:9). As we follow his story, we see that Joshua was a loyal, humble, and obedient disciple to Moses. To me, their relationship resembled that of a father and son, which may be why the story meant so much to me growing up.

While researching the relationship between Joshua and Moses, I found images of a fifteenth-century stained-glass panel of the two of them. It shows Joshua hanging back while Moses led him by the hand. The image is powerful because it illustrates how much Joshua must have admired and looked up to Moses. I'm sure he wanted to be like his mentor, but because Joshua was human, I imagine he felt unqualified and lacking at times. He likely assumed he was inferior to Moses. These are just guesses, but we can see hints in the Bible that Joshua struggled with feeling insufficient and incapable.

There's an interesting exhortation given by God to Joshua, right after he became the leader of all Israel and just prior to leading Israel into the promised land. It was a critical moment in the journey of Joshua's leadership. Moses had just died, so Joshua no longer had his mentor and leader. Meanwhile, the people were looking to him to lead them into battle against impossible odds. God spoke these words to Joshua:

> *Be strong and courageous,* because you will lead these people to inherit the land I swore to their ancestors to give them. *Be strong and very courageous.* Be careful to obey all the law my servant Moses gave you; do not turn from it to the right or to the left, that you may be successful wherever you go. ... Have I not commanded you? *Be strong and courageous.* Do not be afraid; do not be discouraged, for the LORD your God will be with you wherever you go. (Josh. 1:6–7, 9, my emphasis)

In just a few verses, God tells Joshua to be "strong and courageous" three times.

Why would God repeat himself like that? What point was he trying to get across? Hadn't Joshua already proven that he was strong and courageous on the battlefield? Did Joshua feel like he was lacking, even though he seemed to have unshakable faith?

I wonder if it was because Joshua was no different than us. Maybe he struggled with comparing himself to those before him.

Maybe he felt like he couldn't live up to the expectations placed on him.

Maybe he assumed that no matter what he did, he would never be as great as Moses.

Maybe he was afraid the task ahead was beyond his abilities and he would let everyone down.

I think God was speaking directly to Joshua's biggest fear: being incapable of doing what God had called him to do. God wanted Joshua to lead his people into the promised land, which was something that everyone had thought Moses was going to do. But that huge task had fallen to Joshua instead. God wanted to remind Joshua that he could do this, because God was with him—but fear could stop him, if he let it.

In these verses, God was affirming that Joshua was capable of leading the Israelites to complete victory. Yes, Moses led the Israelites out of Egypt and into the desert, but their journey wasn't complete. They had a long way to go!

The problem wasn't that the journey was incomplete; it was that the leader felt incomplete. The skills, abilities, or resources he thought he was lacking made him feel incapable of leading the Israelites on this massive journey, but God wanted him to know that he was complete and that God would use him to bring Israel's journey to completion.

God does the same with us. He always wants to bring something to completion both in us and through us. He wants to make us whole in the areas where we're lacking.

We Are Empowered by God

Just as fear could have held me back from my calling, it could have done the same for Joshua. But he was marked by God and called by God, and he was able to find his power in him. Moses even gave him the name Joshua, which means "The Lord saves." Joshua knew how to trust God, and that made all the difference. I believe that Joshua was only able to save Israel *after* God saved him from his fear of not being enough.

At the end of the day, the Israelites weren't victorious because of Joshua's training, experience, or strength. I mentioned earlier that he was known as a strong military leader, but he wasn't born that way. He was actually born into slavery. But Joshua learned to be confident in a perfectly powerful God. And in the areas where he was lacking in experience and ability, he knew that God would show up.

We all have fears, insecurities, and flaws, but we weren't meant to place our identities on them. We were meant to identify with God and what he says about us. No one is perfect, but we have a God who takes our weaknesses and flaws and infuses his power into them. He births greatness and fullness out of our limitations.

If you feel overwhelmed by the task ahead of you, or if you feel inadequate in the face of impending challenges, let this verse serve as an encouragement: "It has taught us to lose all faith in ourselves and to place all of our trust in the God who raises the dead" (2 Cor. 1:9 TPT).

Through God and his power, and only through that, we are victorious. Our failures are a reminder of our dependency, and that's a good thing. God *wants* us to lose faith in ourselves so that we become more reliant on him.

Many things can leave us feeling lacking. But with God, we can place that feeling in his hands—the same hands that raise the dead. We don't step forward because we're talented and capable. We step forward because of the one who calls and equips us.

Later in the same book, Paul emphasizes the principle Joshua learned: God's power is more than enough in our weakness. Paul had repeatedly prayed for deliverance from an unspecified issue that was limiting him. But instead of granting him a miracle, God granted him grace. Paul describes God's answer to him this way:

> Each time he said, "My grace is all you need. My power works best in weakness." So now I am glad to boast about my weaknesses, so that the power of Christ can work through me. (2 Cor. 12:9 NLT)

In other words, our lack is not a source of shame but of joy. It's an opportunity to trust in God and celebrate his strength. It's a chance to remind ourselves and everyone else that we walk by faith, in grace, not by our own efforts or abilities.

Joshua seems to have learned this lesson well, because he led Israel to victory after victory for decades. He successfully guided Israel into the promised land. He defeated kings, armies, giants, and cities. On one occasion, he even defied the laws of nature and commanded the sun to stand still (Josh. 10:1–15). Joshua consistently had great faith in the face of great odds. Why? Because he knew that in whatever he lacked, God was more than capable of making up the difference. It wasn't his job to figure out how to win the battles, it was his job to trust in God, to believe in himself, and to take faith steps forward.

The same holds true for our generation, and it holds true for you. In our lack, God is an infallible and unlimited source of power and strength.

We Are Accompanied by God

God's presence is the underlying and all-encompassing thing that makes everything else work.

After affirming his presence and power, God told Joshua to enter the promised land and begin the conquest. The first step was to cross the Jordan River, which was overflowing its banks because it was flood season.

That means God's instruction to Joshua followed this progression:

1. Know that I am with you.
2. Be strong and courageous.
3. Step out into the Jordan.

God didn't start by sending Joshua and Israel into a raging river or the thick of battle. He started by affirming his ongoing presence and power. Joshua was encouraged to be strong and courageous by knowing that God would never leave him, and that presence was all he needed, even if he didn't feel like he measured up to human expectations.

God does the same thing for us.

1. God is with us.
2. God makes us strong.
3. God challenges us to step out.

Comparison and lack may cause you to become paralyzed and shrink back from what God calls you to do. So before you step out, you need to be strong. And in order to be strong, you need God's presence and power.

What is holding you back from stepping out? Where are you allowing your feelings to compromise your trust in God? In what areas are you still relying on yourself, instead of stepping out with the strength of God surging through you? God gives you the same exhortation that he gave Joshua: You may be afraid but know that my presence is *always* with you.

No matter what you face, you aren't alone, and you aren't in charge. God is with you, and God is leading you. That is all you need to be victorious.

We Are Equipped by God

God doesn't do everything for us, but he trains us and teaches us to follow his calling for our life. The power is still his, of course, but there is a responsibility on our shoulders to walk in the grace, skill, and wisdom we receive from God. In other words, we have to do the work he equips us to do.

In my case—though this is probably true for many others as well—my limitations weren't my biggest problem. It was my tendency to get in my own way. And I usually did that by getting in my own head.

For example, I took special education reading and writing classes until ninth grade. I don't think I finished a book from cover to cover until after I graduated high school (don't tell my literature teachers). Yet here I am, only a few years later, writing a book of my own. The difference from where I was then to where I am now is almost humorous.

So what happened? I wasn't granted divine literary abilities, that's for sure. I just kept pushing forward over time, learning new things, and saying yes to opportunities to grow. I stopped saying no to things I thought I couldn't do. And more than anything, I began to agree with what God says about me, not about what my feelings of lack tried to tell me.

None of this happened overnight. Actually, it happened as a result of my struggles. That's an important point. I am thankful for the struggles I experienced because they taught me to push past my own limitations and rely on God.

As I look back at the last few years and see the areas where God has changed me and used me, he alone gets the credit. The Bible talks about how God will use the foolish things to confound the wise and the weak things to shame the strong (1 Cor. 1:27). That is certainly my story, and maybe it's yours too.

We need to understand that we don't write our story, Jesus does. You can't rely on you because you will fail you. You need him and his power to succeed in life.

This is why I love how God finished his statement to Joshua in Joshua 1:9. God tells him that he will always be by his side. We've judged ourselves against the people around us too many times rather than taking a second to step back and listen to the God we serve. Joshua seems to have believed he would never live up to Moses's leadership, but he was looking at it all wrong. He was looking at people's perceptions of him, not God's.

It is the same with our limitations and obstacles. We get in our own heads and hinder our own progress when we focus so much on the problem. I've heard it said that rather than telling God how big our problem is, we should tell our problem how big our God is. The same goes for our weaknesses, our insufficiencies, and our lack. God is bigger.

I think we see this demonstrated best through Paul. Before his conversion experience, he was full of himself, and understandably so. He was well-versed in Scripture, held a very respectable position among the Pharisees at a young age, and was respected by the Jews.

But when he came face-to-face with Jesus on the road to Damascus, he realized who he needed to put his confidence in. Throughout his life, Paul continued to grow in humility. His early writings began by saying, "I am the least of the apostles" (1 Cor. 15:9). Further into his walk with Jesus he said, "I am the very least of all the saints" (Eph. 3:8 ESV). Then at the end of his life he said, "Christ Jesus came into the world to save sinners—of whom I am the worst" (1 Tim. 1:15).

This was the man who wrote half of the New Testament, performed phenomenal miracles, and established churches throughout the known world. He did all these things, yet at the end of his life, he called himself the least of all! We see the reason why in a very popular verse.

> I can do all things through Christ who strengthens me. (Phil. 4:13 NKJV)

Notice that Paul didn't say Christ does all things. He said he, *Paul*, can do all things, but he does them *through* Christ. Paul grew in confidence throughout his life, but it wasn't a confidence rooted in his own ability. It was confidence in the one he served. He decreased to make room for God to increase in his life. Yes, he worked hard, he learned new skills, he put himself at risk, he asked for help, he stayed up late and got up early, and he did a million other things to carry out God's will. But he never lost sight of the fact that God was the source of his strength and ability.

My prayer for our generation is that we would understand that our transformation and our calling will not come about through our power but by God's Spirit within us. We must realize that complacency is not an option and arrogance is not the solution. We have to depend on God in our lack, find our completeness in him, and then step into our calling.

So take heart and have courage, because in God, you are fully equipped for whatever you go through. Not because of some special skill or talent, not because you have earned anything by your own merit, not because you have everything figured out—but because of the one who is with you.

It's time to stop looking at what you lack and start believing you are complete in Jesus. He completes you, make you whole, empowers you, accompanies you, and equips you.

Stop finding reasons to feel incomplete and start focusing on God, the only one who is perfect. Lack is not your destiny, so shake off the doubts and negativity and trust in the fullness God provides.

WE ARE A COMPLETE GENERATION,

NOT A LACKING GENERATION.

WE ARE MADE WHOLE IN LOVE,

EMPOWERED BY GRACE,

AND CALLED TO VICTORY IN CHRIST.

EIGHT

You can't change what you refuse to confront.

Unknown

ADDICTION CAN BE A SCARY WORD for a lot of people. It's a label we tend to think applies to people who have hit rock bottom in life and people whose substance abuse or obsession has cost them a great deal.

On the other hand, it's also a word that gets thrown around loosely at times with people claiming (or even boasting) they're #addicted to everything from binge-watching TV shows to drinking five cups of coffee a day.

Our generation has been labeled "addicted." Due to our obsessions with our cell phones, success, and our image, people tend to think millennials are hopelessly lost in addiction.

In my opinion, *addicted* can be one of the easiest labels to ignore and one of the hardest to identify. So what does it really mean to be addicted to something? Let's look at the definition.

Addicted (adj): exhibiting a compulsive, chronic, physiological or psychological need for a habit-forming substance, behavior, or activity.[1]

To be addicted to something means you have a deep need—whether mental or physical—to do something or ingest something. I'm not talking about a superficial "need" such as scrolling through social media or eating an entire box of cookies, but a need or habit that essentially controls you. One that changes your behavior whether you like it or not. Maybe it's sinful or illegal, or maybe it's not. The point is that it has taken over part of your life, typically in a self-destructive way.

Even if the addiction isn't wrong in itself, the excess and the control it has over you usually become a negative. In other words, although not all addictions will land you in jail or rehab, many of them will lead you to a different form of bondage if left unaddressed.

We'll get into some examples as we go along, but first of all, a word of caution. Even if you aren't dealing with some form of addiction right now, keep reading! Avoid the temptation to skip this chapter, because what we will talk about will help you identify addiction, avoid getting caught in its trap, and relate to people who are struggling with it.

Addiction is one of those uncomfortable topics that most of us would rather not talk about. The danger in ignoring addiction, though, is that we end up stigmatizing it. We make it sound like only a small few struggle with it, and if you are one of those few, "shame on you." As a result, those who most need help are too embarrassed to ask for it. But the truth is, addiction is a very real issue for a lot of people, and it is far more damaging when left unaddressed.

Addiction is a struggle within the church too. I think we all know that, even if we rarely talk about it. I read a statistic recently that 68 percent of Christian men watch pornography on a regular basis. That number jumps to 76 percent for men between the ages of eighteen to twenty-four.[2]

Part of the problem is that accessibility to pornographic materials has increased dramatically in the last few years. A few decades ago, pornography was hidden within magazines and adult-rated movies. But today, the average age when a child is introduced to pornography is between the ages of eight and eleven years old, because pornography is essentially E-rated: accessible to everyone.[3] Never before has a generation of men *and* women had greater access to such damaging content. We are just a few clicks, swipes, or likes away from stumbling upon porn, whether intentionally or unintentionally.

Pornography is only one concerning addiction for this generation. We can also become addicted to technology. As a generation that has grown up in a digital, media-saturated world, we don't just use technology as a means of communication or source of information but as a social crutch. It's such a quick form of entertainment that it can displace face-to-face conversations, hobbies, and other elements of a healthy, active lifestyle. One study showed that the average millennial checks their phone 150 times a day.[4] Can you think of anything else you do 150 times a day? According to research by the Nielsen Company, the average young adult spends 43 percent of their time consuming content on digital platforms.[5]

Porn consumption and technology use are only two of the many possible addictions facing our generation. But rather than trying to list out what the rest could be, I want to look at how addiction begins. If we can identify how addiction works, we can take steps to avoid falling into its trap.

SURVIVAL MODE

I'm not an addiction expert or a psychologist, but I've dealt with my share of addictive tendencies and many of my peers have been open with me about some of their struggles. Part of my journey toward freedom was learning everything I could about how addictions work.

This is important, because addictions get their power, in part, from real human needs. So calling us an "addicted generation" is partly true, because we have attempted to meet genuine needs with superficial solutions. But as we've seen throughout this book, God's original design for us is what matters most, and his calling in our lives is bigger and more real than labels like this one. Our tendency toward addictive, destructive behavior, therefore, is not who we are or who we must become. Rather, it is a reminder to return to God's original design and discover his calling.

So how do addictions begin? They rarely, if ever, start on purpose. We don't just wake up one morning and randomly decide "Today I'm going to start a pattern of self-destructive behavior." Addiction is far more subtle than that, and far better disguised.

This behavior often develops out of feelings of neglect, fear, or pressure. When these emotions overwhelm us, our brain switches to survival mode. In this fight-or-flight state, it looks for ways to alleviate stress and return to normal. The part of our brain that is responsible for these emotions is also responsible for our capacity for pleasure. So when we feel neglected, fearful, or pressured, our brain reacts with a craving for pleasure. In other words, when we feel a craving, our brain is actually trying to help us survive.

The problem is, things like food, sex, alcohol, and other forms of quick pleasure can develop into addictions when our natural, necessary human instinct to cope is paired with the wrong coping mechanism. That is, just because our brain creates a craving doesn't mean that craving is actually helpful or healthy.

The things we continuously choose to satisfy our craving for pleasure over pain will become the things our brain convinces us we need. Some things are almost immediately addictive, like certain drugs. But nearly anything can become an addiction if our brain becomes convinced that we need it to be happy.

Here's the really tricky part. Because our brain is telling us that we *need* a particular substance or activity, we often don't recognize it as addiction. It feels logical to us. We find ways to justify it. And instead of giving us reasons to stop the behavior, our brain encourages us to continue it. In a misguided attempt to bring peace, it tries to restore equilibrium to our stressed, pressured lives through moments of pleasure. That doesn't work, of course. But in the moment of temptation, when both your body and brain are trying to convince you to do something, it's very difficult to resist.

And because our brains are in survival mode, we are often unaware (or unwilling to admit) how destructive our behavior is or how it affects people around us. When we are just trying to survive, it's harder to have empathy for others, because we feel an urgent, desperate need to attend to ourselves. All our focus is inward, on survival. But that "survival" is hurting us and those around us.

A TEMPORARY FIX

Addiction, once established, is by definition hard to break, because we are literally fighting against ourselves. We can't trust the voice of reason in our heads, because it might be our survival brain speaking. We can't trust our cravings, because they might be propagating self-destruction. But we can't resist them either (or so we think), because they are so powerful and so insistent. It feels like a betrayal to ignore them, and it feels like a betrayal to obey them.

The apostle Paul made a statement that I think sums up this internal struggle. He was talking about our human tendency toward sin in general, but his comments sound like a man who understood the power of addiction.

> I want to do what is right, but I can't. I want to do what is good, but I don't. I don't want to do what is wrong, but I do it anyway. (Rom. 7:18–19 NLT)

If you've ever dealt with an addiction, you understand the strange struggle between self-protection and self-destruction, between guilt and desire, between living for the moment and looking toward the future.

Over the past few years, I've had countless conversations with guys who are struggling with addictions, especially porn addictions. And I know for myself what it feels like to be trapped by and addicted to porn. It's so important to me to keep having those conversations and expose porn addiction for what it is because I used to be there.

My addiction to porn began when I was only eleven years old, and it ruthlessly took hold of my life. The first time I looked at porn, I stumbled upon it while surfing the web. At first I was repulsed, and I clicked away from it instantly. But my curiosity got the best of me, and later I went back.

Within a short time, I was completely addicted. I remember the pain I felt every time I looked at it. Not in the moment but afterward. I would get so angry with myself, and I would promise to never do it again—only to go back the next day.

I had never experienced something that could so easily entrap me. I felt weak, powerless, ashamed, and dirty. And at the same time, I felt like a slave. I hated it but I couldn't leave it. I was convinced that pornography was an addiction I couldn't overcome.

I quickly learned that addiction doesn't only affect people who have hit rock bottom, and it isn't something you can casually flirt with. Being caught in addiction is like being in quicksand. It slowly traps you and pulls you in, and when you try to break free, you only struggle helplessly while it continues to drag you under.

Just like many men and women who find themselves in the middle of an addiction, I never thought I'd end up in that state. I didn't go looking for porn; it found me. But I gave in to it because of the pleasure it brought in the moment. And as I was exposed to it more and more, my brain began to see porn as the answer.

I learned that even though our brain feels like it needs something for survival, addiction to the wrong things will only leave us feeling like something is missing. Porn doesn't have the power to fix what is broken or missing in our lives. It can't remove the pressures or the stress. It can't bring lasting happiness or fulfillment.

The same goes for any other addiction, no matter how harmless it might seem. These things are powerless to bring resolution and healing to our hearts. The best they can do is cover up our trauma or stress or fear. They can offer a temporary escape and short-lived relief from our internal pain. But ultimately, they leave us emptier than ever.

FIGHT NOT FLIGHT

I mentioned above that addictions tap into the fight-or-flight impulse of the brain. Because we are living in survival mode, we subconsciously look for ways to either overcome the threat at hand or run away from it.

Turning toward cravings, then, is flight. It's escape. It means we don't see any hope of overcoming the threat, so we run the other way and hope to find solace and safety in something else.

I can't say this strongly enough though. God has not called us to flight but to fight. There is no obstacle, no stressful situation, no trauma, no problem, no inner demons too great for him to overcome. If we can grow in our faith in him, we can learn to stand our ground and fight.

We fight addiction.

We fight unhealthy cravings.

We fight to control our thoughts.

We fight to overcome temptations.

We fight to rule our feelings and passions.

We fight against whatever tries to control us.

We fight to overcome stress, pressure, and tension.

We fight to be strong, mature, balanced children of God.

We do not have to be an addicted generation; we can be a fighting generation. We can be a courageous, committed, tenacious group of people who know our identity and refuse to back down or give in. Rather than caving to our cravings or escaping into pleasure, we can deal with the issues at hand and find true peace.

There is nothing wrong with pleasure, of course. God created us with the capacity to enjoy life, and he gave us food, friendships, love, sex, beauty, and much, much more for our enjoyment.

Our desires and impulses are not right or wrong in themselves—what makes them either good or bad is the way we fulfill them. In his book *Mere Christianity*, C. S. Lewis compares the desires we feel to the notes on a piano. He states that there are not right or wrong notes but rather all notes can be right at one time and wrong at another.

The problem arises when pleasure becomes our strategy for dealing with pressure. That simply doesn't work. We must face pressure with courage and strength. Like soldiers facing an enemy, we must advance toward whatever seems threatening rather than running from it.

Growing up, I always wanted to be a warrior, and I had some epic battles with my brothers to prove it! Now that I'm an adult, I *still* want to be a warrior. And I see an enormous battlefield in front of me and in front of our generation. It's the battle for our future.

I believe our generation wants to be a fighting generation, a group of warriors who persevere toward what they believe in, an army on the same mission. But when it comes time for battle, sometimes flight seems easier than fight.

The battle is certainly not easy. Fighting was a lot simpler when my opponents were my brothers. Don't get me wrong, they would definitely rough me up—but I always knew they would ease up if I was actually getting hurt.

But we're not fighting against an enemy that will ease up. The stakes are higher. The battlefield is rougher. There is no tap out option. Being a warrior requires staying in the fight no matter how rough and painful it gets. It means embracing your war and fighting for your future.

That's how we must approach addictions, it's how we must face temptations, and it's how we must handle the stress and pressure of life that makes us want to run. We have to show up to fight. We have to go to war for ourselves and for the people we love.

WORTH THE FIGHT

The struggle against self-destructive behavior and addictions is not easy. So why fight at all? Wouldn't it be easier to choose the flight option? I see three clear reasons to fight, and I'd like to look briefly at each of them.

1. Fight for Yourself

You are worth more than any addiction will give you. God wants you to have freedom and abundant life. Don't settle for lies that say you don't deserve anything better, that you've already ruined everything, that you're not strong enough to change, or that your life doesn't matter.

I know those lies, because I heard them in my mind. Addiction doesn't play fair. First it enslaves us, then it taunts us. It holds us captive, and then it tells us it's our fault we're there. It tries to convince us that if we were just stronger, we could be free. The fight for freedom is yours to begin, but you have to value yourself enough to swing the first punch.

We've spent the last few chapters looking at how God sees us. We've heard the words he speaks over us and considered the calling he has for us. Use those truths as you fight. Addiction is not who you are—you are who God says you are.

2. Fight for Your Relationship with God

God is for us, he loves us, and he wants nothing more than to have a close, intimate relationship with us. However, even though nothing can separate us from his love, there are things that can block our connection with him. Addiction is one of them.

To be clear, I'm *not* saying that God distances himself from us or that we're no longer Christians when we sin. His grace is always available to us, no matter what we're struggling with. His love never changes, and our salvation and acceptance are secure in him.

As we saw with David's sin in chapter 5, our actions do have consequences, and one of those consequences is a broken relationship with God. Addiction, particularly when the addictive behavior is something the Bible would define as sin, has the power to cause a disconnect between God and us.

We have a covenant relationship with our creator. In the Bible, we're called the bride of Christ, so it makes sense to look at the relationship similar to a marriage. If you were married, and your spouse found out that you were cheating on them repeatedly, do you think they'd feel connected enough to share the intimate secrets of their heart with you? Not a chance!

In the same way, our sin breaks down the intimacy in our relationship with God. He still loves us just as much, despite the mess we make of things, but we pull ourselves further away from his heart when we continue to choose our addiction over him. Unresolved addiction is a powerful, self-defeating weapon that undermines our relationship with God.

3. Fight for Your Future

Addiction breaks the vertical relationship with God, and it also breaks our horizontal relationships with one another. Besides that, it breaks our concentration, steals our resources, distracts our focus, and destroys our self-esteem. Put all those together and it's easy to see why addiction is such a hindrance to our future.

When I was a kid, I always dreamed of my future wife and the marriage we'd have. I imagined being someone who would fight for my marriage and never do anything to hurt it. But one day I realized I was doing that very thing every time I looked at pornography. With each image, I was damaging my relationship with my future spouse.

Remember this principle: what we do *now* always affects our *later*.

Most addictions start small, but because they wield power, they lead to trouble. Whether it's porn, alcohol, drugs, food, social media, or success, what begins as something minor can become a monster. Over time, one small thing done repeatedly can have a giant effect on the hopes and dreams we have for our lives.

No one plans on having a bad marriage, broken family, or lost job. But if we hold on to addictions and refuse to give them to God, we begin to compromise our future.

That's the bad news, but here's the good news. God is the restorer of all things! When we give him the things that hold power over us—by confessing them, bringing them into the light, and asking for grace to change—he begins a restoration process that leads to victory.

"Fight the good fight of the faith," Paul told his friend Timothy (1 Tim. 6:12). Faith is more than just believing the gospel; it's believing that God is with us and for us, and that in him we have abundant life.

Fight for yourself, fight for your relationship with God, and fight for your future. Breaking free from addiction is always a war. But it's a fight you can win.

DON'T FIGHT ALONE

So how do we break free from the things that hold us captive? How do we overcome addiction?

One of the most important steps is also one of the hardest. Don't fight alone.

If you want to break free from quicksand, you have to be aware of what you're caught in. But you also need someone or something stronger to get you out. The same is true for breaking free from addiction. You have to recognize that you're trapped in a negative cycle, and you have to rely on something stronger—God, healthy habits, friends, and family—to pull you out.

I spent the majority of my addiction fighting alone. Why? Because I didn't want to deal with the shame of sharing what I was going through with others. I remember those dark times and how angry I would get with myself for failing yet again. Looking back, I wish I would have brought someone into my mess right away so that I could pick up the phone and talk with them after I had messed up. Instead, I was trapped in a cycle of addiction, failure, and guilt for eight years.

My journey to freedom started with this passage in the New Testament.

> Therefore, confess your sins to one another and pray for one another, that you may be healed. The prayer of a righteous person has great power as it is working. (James 5:16 ESV)

James made a few key points in this verse. First, *confession is powerful.* It opens the door to freedom, because when you confess and receive prayer, you *will* be healed and set free. But if no one ever knows that you're struggling, how can you experience the power of their prayers?

Second, *prayer is powerful.* Prayer has the power to change everything. Why? Because God is powerful, and prayer means turning to God and asking for his grace and aid. When you confess your sins to someone, they stand with you, and when they pray for you, God stands with you too. Three is better than one—especially when one of the three is God!

Third, *the answer to prayer doesn't have a time line.* James didn't say when or how the healing will come. I struggled for years before I finally broke free from my addiction. We don't know the time line, but our job is to confess, pray, and keep fighting. We *will* find freedom if we don't give up or give in.

Finally, *seek help from a righteous person.* In other words, find someone who is following God and has a lifestyle that matches his or her faith. The idea is to speak with someone who can help you, not just someone who can listen to you. This is difficult, because it might seem like it would be easier to tell your best friend. I'm sure your best friend is awesome, but that doesn't mean he or she is the best person to help you fight your battle.

In my case, this step meant talking with a pastor friend of mine at a Bible study I was attending. I remember asking him if I could talk with him alone, then sharing what I was going through. I was unsure how he would respond or if he would immediately tell my parents. But despite my fears, as soon as I told him, I felt a massive weight lifted off my shoulders.

When we open up our hearts to someone, we're not just trusting the person with knowledge of our secret addiction. We're trusting their response. The problem with confiding in someone who's close to us but not necessarily close to God is that, while we can rely on their kindness, we can't necessarily rely on their advice since we don't know if their answer will be based on biblical truth. Righteous people, however, can respond with both kindness *and* godly counsel.

If you're ready for the enemy to lose the power he has over your addiction, shine light on it. Share it with someone who is more mature in faith.

Bringing something into the light allows us to take back the power. The enemy works in the dark. He loves to keep things hidden so that we feel trapped and stuck. When we confess to someone else, it means we no longer have to hide in the dark or carry our burdens alone. When we voice our struggle, our vulnerability allows light to break through.

Remember, breaking free from addiction is a fight. No warrior goes into battle alone. We must invite godly people to fight alongside us, then persevere as long as it takes to win the victory.

FIGHT WITH GRACE

If we are neck deep in addiction, it's easy to forget that God is on our side. We feel so worthless and so ashamed that we don't believe God could possibly still be standing beside us. Addiction and darkness make us feel like God is a million miles away.

But nothing could be further from the truth. God wants to see you freed from your addiction more than you do.

That's why God gives us grace. Grace is not just about God forgiving us for our sins. If it were, we would be forgiven but doomed to continually fall on our faces. Grace is about God's power working through us to do what we can't do in our human ability: change.

Grace enables us to escape both the guilt and the power of sin.

Remember what Paul said about grace in weakness? We looked at this in the last chapter.

Each time he said, "My grace is all you need. My power works best in weakness." So now I am glad to boast about my weaknesses, so that the power of Christ can work through me. (2 Cor. 12:9 NLT)

I love the first two lines. Where we are weakest, grace is strongest. Where we lack the most, God gives the most.

But grace can only function when we allow it to—that is, when we stop trying to do everything on our own. We can't win any battles if we neglect God's grace. We have to believe his power works best in weakness and that his grace has the power to set us free.

On a practical level, fighting with grace means two things. You have

1. an unshakable belief that you are forgiven
2. a tenacious belief that God is helping you change

Both are important. When you fail, you need grace to cover your failure. You are forgiven and accepted by grace and grace alone. Nothing can change that. But you also need grace to stand up again, to try again, to fight again. Fight with grace and grace will fight for you.

FEAR THE RIGHT THING

Along with receiving God's grace in the fight against addiction, we must know how to handle fear. Fear plays a unique role in addiction. When I was addicted to pornography, I was scared that, even if I broke free, I would keep falling back into addiction's trap. And whenever I felt that fear, I stumbled. Why? Because I handed my fear to the wrong master.

Most fears only keep us trapped. Fear of addiction, fear of failure, fear of being caught, fear of punishment—those fears and more will keep us isolated, humiliated, and chained to addiction. Fear has a way of controlling our lives.

Whatever you fear will be the master of your life.

But fear can actually work for us, if we fear the right thing. In my addiction, I realized I needed to change what I feared. I had to retrain myself to fear God more than addiction or temptation. In fact, I had to fear God more than *anything* else in my life.

I'm not talking about terror or about being scared of God. I'm not advocating a fear-based relationship to God or a religion based on threats. I'm talking about the healthy fear of God that the Bible teaches us we should all have. My dad writes about it this way: "the fear of God is not being afraid of him, but being afraid of being away from him."[6]

A healthy fear recognizes the power and goodness of God. It understands the importance of guarding our relationship with him from things that could create distance, as we saw earlier.

The problem with addiction is that not only does it cause there to be distance between God and us but it also fills that distance with things that should have no place in our life: bad habits, unhealthy tendencies, poor decisions, selfish impulses. Those things only reinforce our separation. That is why the Bible says to not just keep a safe distance from these things but to flee from them.

So how does the fear of God help us? Again, whatever we fear will be our master. When we have a proper view of God—his power and goodness, his holiness and mercy—we will run toward him, not away from him. We will flee evil and seek good, because we will value our walk with him and his approval of us more than any temporary pleasure or tantalizing temptation.

FIGHT FOR THE PRIZE

Fleeing temptation and running toward God bring me to the final point I want to make. As you fight the good fight of grace, make sure you are not just running *from* something but running *to* something. In other words, identify the things that will motivate you and empower you to escape the quicksand of addiction. You should run to God first and foremost, of course, but you also need to run toward the future and the promises he has made. Keeping those things in mind will strengthen you in your fight.

I read a book a few years back about someone I truly admire, a man named Louis Zamperini. In the book, Zamperini was a rebel without a cause, someone running hard but with no destination. Then people around him, including his older brother, began to remind him of who he was and what lay ahead of him, and his trajectory changed. He went on to set the national high school track record for the mile, and later he competed as a distance runner in the Olympics.

The story didn't end there though. Zamperini became a lieutenant in the army air corps and fought in World War II. His aircraft was downed at sea, and he spent several weeks adrift in a life raft, only to be captured by the Japanese and held as a prisoner of war. After surviving imprisonment and beatings, he returned home to a hero's welcome. Years later, he became a Christian, and went on to minister to at-risk youth for many years. He passed away in 2014.[7]

Zamperini's life was a vivid, inspiring testament to his determination to run toward something: not just Olympic glory but survival in impossible circumstances, victory, and the pursuit of helping others. A phrase in his book, *The Devil at My Heels*, sums up his attitude toward hardship: "I'd made it this far and refused to give up because all my life I had always finished the race."[8]

Before running a race or starting a fight, we have to know what we are aiming for. Zamperini ran for a medal and then for freedom. For those of us who find ourselves in addiction, we must run toward the promises of God.

Some of the promises I believe God wants to fulfill in your life include

- to be an overcomer
- to experience freedom
- to have an abundant life
- to have great relationships
- to be part of a healthy family
- to be successful in his calling for you

A good father wants good things for his children, and God wants the best things for us. Because we are new creations, and because God's nature is to win, victory is the destiny waiting for us. The only way we can lose is if we stop fighting.

This is our battle plan. I'm not saying that if you do these things, you'll instantly break free. If you did, that would be awesome, and God would deserve gratitude and praise. But for most of us, this will be a fierce fight. Wars are rarely won overnight but, instead, through a series of battles.

Remember, though, you have a calling from God, and it is *not* to be addicted. You have been set apart by God as his special treasure. He values you, he loves you, and he fights alongside you.

When we were growing up, my mom gave us boys a challenge: To live set apart. We knew we were called to live differently. We watched friends and even church leaders do questionable things and get away with it. We wondered why they were able to slide by without punishment. But my mom always told us that the call upon our lives was too important for us to mimic what we saw. Because of that challenge, we had to say no to some things that others said yes to. We wanted to be set apart in God's eyes, not the world's. We wanted to live free.

This is the charge I want to speak over your life: to live set apart. There is a call on your life, but it's up to you to walk in it instead of away from it. You have to make the choice not to tiptoe near the line, treating temptation casually. You have to choose to follow a secure path that will inspire and lead others. You might have heard the saying, if you don't stand for something, you'll fall for anything. In other words, choose to live for something. Set a standard for yourself based on integrity and calling, and live set apart for God.

God has given us everything we need to fight well. He is calling us to remove the label of "addicted" and be a generation set apart. He wants us to live for things beyond this world so that we can walk freely in the life he has given us now. Now it's up to us to fight for that calling.

WE ARE A **FIGHTING** GENERATION,

NOT AN ADDICTED GENERATION.

NOTHING CONTROLS US.

NO ONE OWNS US.

WE SERVE GOD ALONE,

AND IN HIM, WE FIND FREEDOM.

NINE

DISCOURAGED

We must accept finite disappointment, but never lose infinite hope.

Martin Luther King Jr.

THINK OF THE BIGGEST DREAM you've ever dared to dream. Remember the courage it took to begin dreaming, the obstacles you overcame in your mind to build hope around that idea, the emotion you poured into every thought associated with it.

Now, imagine that dream has suddenly been crushed. Think of the gut-wrenching feeling you would experience when reality comes crashing down on your goals and visions.

That feeling is *discouragement,* and if we're not careful, it can steal not only our dreams but our hope, joy, and future too.

Discouragement can be defined in many different ways, but this definition from *The Dictionary of Bible Themes* expresses it clearly.

A sense of unhappiness arising from a loss of confidence in one's own abilities, in the reliability of God or in the power of the gospel. Discouragement can occur in the Christian life, especially when there is resistance to the gospel or in instances of personal failure.[1]

I can definitely relate to that definition. I remember one of the first times I spoke at a church. Before I began, I was confident in my speaking ability—but I was in for a rude awakening. I got up before the audience and forgot most of my notes. I have blurry memories of standing there in terror, drenched in sweat, rambling through what little I could remember. I had forty minutes to speak but finished in fifteen.

Afterward, I was so discouraged! My expectations about my abilities were shattered. My dad was at the service, and we had a conversation later. He explained to me that he doesn't rely on his own speaking ability but rather on God. When he speaks, his confidence is in the Holy Spirit working through him. That made an impact on me, because I had just seen what happened when I got up there without any prayer or any real attempt to let the Holy Spirit work through me. I decided right then, *never again*!

Discouragement floods into our lives when our outcomes are different from our expectations. That's why disappointment follows broken dreams. Our dreams carry a set of hopes, beliefs, and expectations.

These feelings of discouragement often accompany seasons of life when we aren't accomplishing what we set out to do or our lives don't look the way we'd hoped. Those disappointments make it difficult to fight off a spirit of pessimism. It can hit us when people we love hurt or leave us. It can strike when our business or our marriage or our ministry seems to be falling apart around us. When expectations are not fulfilled for a prolonged period of time, discouragement naturally follows.

The scary thing is that discouragement can be a self-propagating monster. The more we allow it to prosper, the more it takes on a life of its own. Psychologist Margaret Wehrenberg writes this:

> As people feel discouraged, they slip into a habit of negative thoughts—getting into a "rut" that is literally descriptive of brain function. Any time that you repeatedly think the same thought, your brain recognizes that as significant and tries to help you out. It begins making it easier to think that negative thought by providing more blood supply and white matter to speed up processing. Thus, depressed mood and thinking increases in a vicious circle, and finding a pathway out of it gets harder and harder.[2]

The opposite is true as well, of course. If we consistently meditate on hope-filled thoughts, we will predispose our brain toward positivity and optimism. The problem is that life presents us many opportunities to become discouraged, and if we don't process them correctly, we can end up filling our minds with this self-propagating negativity.

When you were younger, you likely had dreams for your future. You may have pictured the job you'd have, the person you'd marry, or the impact you'd have on the world around you. You may have even prayed for those things and asked God to reveal them to you. But over time, it's possible that something happened to crush those dreams.

Our generation tends to have huge expectations for the future. We imagine that something grand must be waiting for us around every corner. We were told we can do whatever we set our minds to, and we believed those words.

But once we stepped into the real world, we realized something: the people who pumped up the possibilities of our remarkable future failed to warn us about the unremarkable challenges we'd face along the way. Instead of conquering the world, we are left conquering college debt. Before we can make any grand discoveries, we have to discover how to pay the rent. The things we once dreamed of seem further away than ever from our reality. And as a result, we are discouraged.

God does not call us to be a discouraged generation though. He didn't create us to live in disappointment or to define ourselves by the dreams we never achieved. Instead of being discouraged, we are called to be a hopeful generation.

The apostle Paul wrote to the Ephesians about their calling in Jesus. Notice the phrasing he chose.

I pray that your hearts will be flooded with light so that you can understand the confident hope he has given to those he called—his holy people who are his rich and glorious inheritance. (1:18 NLT)

Did you catch that? Paul's prayer was that they would understand, believe, and live out the "confident hope [God] has given to those he called."

As a generation and as individuals, we must shake off the negative label of discouraged and instead embrace our calling to hope. Not a hope based in our own abilities or in the world around us or in another human being but a hope in Christ.

LOSING HOPE

The reason our hope in Christ matters so much is because hope placed in anything else will ultimately disappoint us. That's why we feel discouraged so often—our hopes have been dashed by things that are unworthy.

When the world crushes our dreams—or when debt and dreary jobs chip away at them slowly—it's natural to feel hopeless. Trust me, I've been there! Day-to-day routine starts to displace dreams, high expectations are replaced with reality, and hope gives way to discouragement.

If you are dealing with discouragement or loss of hope in some area, ask yourself this: Who let me down?

Maybe it was a career, a job, or a boss.

Maybe it was a church or a pastor.

Maybe it was a significant other.

Maybe it was the economy.

Maybe it was a parent.

Maybe it was God.

That last one might sound odd, but many people are disappointed by God. Or better said, by unfulfilled *expectations* of God. They were praying for a healing or waiting on his provision or fighting for restoration in their family and God didn't respond the way they expected. If that's you, it's important to recognize that feeling for what it is. God isn't offended by your frustration, but he doesn't want you to remain there either.

Regardless of what might have replaced our dreams with cynicism, recognizing who has let us down—where our hope has been placed—is crucial in identifying where discouragement started.

Hope is powerful, because it's the thing that pulls us through when nothing else seems to work. It's the force that guides us forward when everything is working against us. It's the saving grace when hardships push us further than we thought we could go.

But if our hope rests on something that can't support our dreams or sustain our future, then we are hoping in the wrong thing and we are setting ourselves up for discouragement.

One of the most common reasons our hopes get dashed is because we often attach them to another person, such as a spouse, a parent, a boss, or even friends. Humans are the most unpredictable variable on this planet! Even those with the best intentions fall short of perfection. We can't hang our hopes on fallible human beings.

When I was young, my family moved from Florida to Colorado to be a part of an amazing church. We loved the pastor and appreciated his incredible leadership. He became like a second father to me and my brothers. Naturally, we placed high expectations on him and his behavior.

Unfortunately, when I was twelve years old, we learned this man had had a moral failure. It came as a complete shock to our family. We were devastated and discouraged. Even though we weren't directly affected by the issue at hand, the high expectations we had of him made it feel like a personal blow.

When our parents talked to my brothers and me about the situation, they told us they were worried that his failure might affect our faith. My oldest brother said something in response that has stuck with me to this day. "We're fine. We're all sad about what happened, but our pastor didn't die on a cross for us. Jesus did. So we're all going to be okay." My brother didn't put his hope in a person on earth. He put his hope in the divine person of Jesus.

I'm not saying we should distrust everyone or be cynical about all leadership but identifying the source of our discouragement or hope should ultimately lead us to Jesus. He is the only one worthy of our absolute confidence.

POWER IN THE PROCESS

The Bible records a story about a woman named Hannah who was unable to have children. Her story can be found in 1 Samuel 1–2, and if you read it, you'll notice that Hannah is first described as being entirely focused on having a baby the natural way. She was so fixated on the process that it was affecting her marriage, her health, and her emotions.

What Hannah didn't know, though, was that God was going to answer her prayer eventually, but there was a process that needed to take place first. She was so focused on her inability to have a son that she became discouraged by her circumstances, and she let that discouragement keep her from worshiping God in the waiting because she couldn't see him moving.

Focusing on what we're missing causes us to miss out on what God is doing. When we are in that place of discouragement, we may start thinking that our present reality is all that is ever going to exist. We stop believing God will work on our behalf, and we start believing we must settle. Hardships make us so focused on our lack of control in our circumstances that we turn our attention away from the incredible power of God and the process of growth he is putting us through.

Scripture says God closed Hannah's womb, which means that she was barren. In other words, she didn't do this to herself, it wasn't her fault, and she couldn't control it. But the real point is this: God can control the things we cannot.

I believe God does the same with us sometimes. He places us in a season of barrenness and discouragement in some area of our life, and we are unable to produce fruit or find hope in our circumstances.

That may feel strange to you. You may be thinking, *Why would God choose to make his people barren? Why would he put us in a season of hardship? Doesn't he want us to flourish, dream, and produce fruit?*

Of course he does! But I think it's important to remember that life is a process, and ultimately, God knows the steps we must take far better than we do. He knows when we have lessons to learn, character to build, and faith to develop. There are some lessons that can only be learned through trials, but there are incredible blessings and promises on the other side.

It's good to envision the miraculous, incredible things we're expecting from God, but we can't forget to envision the process that comes before them. Our generation has to embrace the idea that there is power in the process.

Allowing something to develop over time isn't a popular concept with people our age. We like things that are instantaneous. We want immediate results. It's what we've become conditioned to expect.

If we want to get in touch with a friend, we just pick up our phones.

If we want to know who'd win in a fight between Batman and Superman, Google gives us an instant answer (FYI—it's always Batman).

If we want to see what our friends are up to, we can jump on social media.

If we want coffee, we can have it waiting for us when we arrive with just a few taps on the Starbucks app.

If we're hungry, we don't even have to leave our house. We can order whatever we are craving and it'll be at our door in minutes.

The problem is we don't just want instant results with people, information, food, and social media. We also want instant results with our dreams. So when our dreams are being shaped and refined through a slow process, it's easy to become discouraged. This is when we begin to think, *Wait a minute. This isn't the way life is supposed to work. This isn't the way I pictured it in my mind.*

Instead of feeling limited by the process, let's lean into it. Use the times of waiting to fan the passion within you and to prepare yourself for a spiritual breakthrough.

Yes, sometimes our dreams take time. And yes, sometimes we have to simply endure the process. But God is always trying to do something *in* us in order to do something *through* us. The barren seasons of life can develop our character in a powerful way, and that character will protect and carry us toward our dreams.

DESPERATE FOR GOD

The most important part of this process is the growth it produces in our relationship with God. When we are discouraged, frustrated, or confused, we will (hopefully) find ourselves turning to our creator. Since we are out of control, we look to the one who controls the universe.

Early in her story, when Hannah was discouraged by the reality of her barrenness, she didn't seek God and instead was caught up in human effort, struggles, and even conflict. Aren't you and I prone to do the same thing? In seasons of discouragement, we try to resolve our frustrations by taking them out on other people or fixing them in our own strength. The problem is, neither of those things will sustain our hope or have the power to fix whatever is discouraging us.

When Hannah drew back, her husband, Elkanah, tried to comfort her. He said, "Why be downhearted just because you have no children? You have me—isn't that better than having ten sons?" (1 Sam. 1:8 NLT).

Sorry, Elkanah, but even though my wife and I don't have kids, I'm smart enough to know that a statement like that won't ease the pain! Why? Because a substitute is not enough. When God has given us a dream, we have a hard time settling for anything less.

That doesn't mean we don't try though. In the face of discouragement, we often attempt to find something to replace the dream or distract us from our frustration. That "something" represents the real danger of discouragement. It can lure us to settle for a substitute that doesn't come from God.

Whether it's drugs, alcohol, relationships, achievement,

money, image, or something else, discouragement can leave us vulnerable to settling for temporary relief instead of finding lasting hope in God. When we feel like giving in to that search for satisfaction, we have to keep running to God in the midst of our discouragement.

The key to fighting discouragement is to let it turn you toward God. That was what Hannah eventually did.

Being barren discouraged her, but it didn't cause her to lose sight of her dreams. Even through her disappointment, she remembered God's promises and his goodness. After wrestling with discouragement, she turned to God. She went to the temple and cried out with everything she had for God to open her womb.

We have the same choice. We can either run to what society says is good enough or we can cry out to God and place total dependence on him.

The idea of crying out to God with everything you have sounds poetic, but please realize that Hannah was releasing a desperate cry from her soul, from her pain, from the darkness of impossibility and hopelessness. When you are in circumstances that create such a desperation, there is nothing poetic about it.

But the desperation can work for you if you know where to turn for hope. Seasons of discouragement lead us to desperation for God. Let that desperation drive you to the one who controls your future.

DREAMING IN THE DARK

In her desperation, Hannah went to the temple and prayed fervently. She wept so intensely that the priest, Eli, thought she was drunk. Instead of being offended by the accusation, she explained that she was begging for God's aid.

> I am very discouraged, and I was pouring out my heart to the LORD. Don't think I am a wicked woman! For I have been praying out of great anguish and sorrow. (1 Sam. 1:15–16 NLT)

Eli realized that she was having a moment with God, and he encouraged her in her pursuit.

> Go in peace, and may the God of Israel grant you what you have asked of him. (v. 17)

This is where the story takes a dramatic turn. Hannah's power was limited, but God's power was not. Hannah could have stayed focused on her circumstances, but instead, she leaned into God. In her darkest hour, she began to dream again. She saw beyond her limitations and trusted in God, and she found faith to hope again.

The same hope is available to us as well.

Maybe you're going through a hard time at work. Maybe you're in a difficult relationship. Maybe school has been overwhelming. And although you cry out to God, maybe it feels like nothing is happening. In those barren seasons of discouragement, when your dreams seem to be stuck in a rut, it's easy to feel as if God isn't listening. If that's where you're at, draw hope from Hannah's story. You might be at the end of your strength, but he is just getting started.

The best part of this story is that not only was God about to answer Hannah's prayer, he was also going to give her even more than she dreamed of. She thought she wanted a son for herself, but the child God had planned for her was Samuel, one of the greatest leaders in Israel's history. And the blessing didn't stop there. God was going to give her three more sons and two daughters.

Hannah didn't realize that God was dreaming bigger dreams than she was. She would have been happy with one son, but she didn't realize the result of her process, her prayers, and her faith would be six kids, one of whom would lead Israel faithfully as a priest and prophet for many years. If she had let discouragement keep her from God's promises, it would have changed her life and the future of Israel altogether.

God's dreams are always bigger than ours. He's *always* working in our lives, even when the process seems slow or halted.

Hannah is a great example of how releasing discouragement and embracing hope can change the trajectory of our lives. We will have plenty of opportunities to be discouraged. Hardships will come up against our dreams. We will face failure, and it will be painful. People will let us down, and it will test us to the core. But we must stand firm in our faith, even in our darkest hour. We cannot let discouragement get us down. Instead, it should drive us toward God and the hope of our calling in him.

If you and I are going to welcome God's best for our future and the future of others, our hope has to lie in Christ. Jesus is our hope for everything. He will never let us down. Although discouragement may come our way, as long as our hope is in him, it will not remain! No matter how long our dreams are delayed or how far short our expectations seem to fall, we will *always* have hope.

Our generation can be hopeful because of God's calling, not because of our strength. While the world around us accepts discouragement as a way of life, we can flip the narrative. We can be overcomers and world changers. Instead of letting discouragement knock us on our face in defeat, let it push us to our knees in prayer, where we can fight even harder. Let's be a generation that dares to hope, even in our darkest hours.

WE ARE A HOPEFUL GENERATION,

NOT A DISCOURAGED GENERATION,

OUR HOPE IS IN JESUS.

HIS CALLING IS OUR FUTURE,

AND IN HIM, OUR DREAMS WILL COME TRUE.

TEN

What separates privilege from entitlement is gratitude.

Brené Brown

IN ANCIENT ISRAEL, the hierarchy of kingship typically played out through a king's descendants, similar to royalty today. A king's eldest son would assume the throne at the proper time, then his son after him, and so on. This was the system followed for many centuries. The royal birthright and title belonged to the heir to the throne.

The same holds true today. There is an entitlement that comes from royal birth. Being born into royalty carries with it a range of rights, duties, honors, titles, and expectations (along with more than a few tabloid stories). In this context, to be entitled is not a negative label but a statement of fact. It simply means members of the royal family receive certain things due to who they are.

But what happens when the appropriate title, honor, or power is not enough for someone? What happens when those born into greatness want more than is rightfully theirs?

That is the dark side of entitlement, and the most famous Israelite king, David, had to deal with it with one of his sons. The story is found in 2 Samuel 15–18. David's son Absalom was handsome, smooth-talking, and popular with the people. Because of these things, he thought he should be king instead of his father. But he wasn't the rightful heir—the throne had been promised to Solomon.

Absalom's pride and immaturity created a sense of entitlement in his heart. This caused him to lose focus on what was already his and to become envious of something not meant for him. Absalom began a rebellion against his own father, which brought great shame and division to his family. Ultimately, the army Absalom led in opposition to the throne was defeated, and while attempting to flee, he was killed by his father's general.

The story is a sad, complicated tale of violence, betrayal, and death. It clearly highlights the dangers associated with a feeling of entitlement and wrongful ambition.

It's important for us to dive into this topic because that's how many people view our generation. They see us as an arrogant, selfish generation who believes we're entitled to anything we desire. Rather than living with contentment and gratitude for what we have, the perception is that we always think we deserve more, that we're never satisfied, and that we seek special treatment or privileges.

Take the workplace, for example. I've seen research that states millennials are one of the hardest generations to employ. Reports say we create problems for the people who hire us, we are difficult to engage with, we don't make long-term commitments, we won't stay at jobs we don't like . . . and the list goes on.

Are those perceptions of our entitled attitudes justified? To be honest, I believe we do have a slight tendency toward entitlement, and we'll look at the reasons for that below.

But we are not called to be an entitled generation. It's not God's design for us, and it's not our identity. So what is our calling? What is God's answer to being entitled?

Our generation must learn to counteract entitlement with gratitude.

Gratitude is simple to understand, and it's not that hard to live out. However, it does take humility, which is not always easy to muster up. And it also takes intentionality, because we have to remind ourselves to be grateful for what we have.

Before we look at how to develop gratitude, let's take a closer look at entitlement. Just as with the other labels we've examined, understanding this word and why it has been used to describe us will help us see God's original design and calling for our generation more clearly.

DON'T CALL ME SPOILED

Absalom was born into privilege, but he let privilege get into his head. Rather than being grateful for what he had, he became greedy for more. In a word, he was spoiled. His entitlement led to wrong expectations, and those expectations ultimately led to his own destruction.

Our generation could be perceived in a similar way—not in the sense of overthrowing anyone's kingdom, hopefully, but in the sense that we have unparalleled privileges and opportunities yet we sometimes struggle to appreciate those privileges and take advantage of the opportunities.

Again, being entitled or spoiled is not God's calling for us, so we need to make sure we avoid the tendencies of Absalom and instead embrace things like gratitude, humility, and hard work. Therefore, I want to briefly look at three reasons we may seem entitled.

Things Have Always Been Instantly Available to Us

We are used to things being available in an instant, as we saw in the last chapter. Friends are just a text away. Answers to our questions are just a Google search away. And while that accessibility isn't a bad thing, it could contribute toward attitudes of impatience, a short attention span, and so forth.

Again, I'm not saying this is who we are. But it's wise to understand our tendencies and how others perceive us so that if we have begun to take on an entitled or ungrateful attitude, we can identify it and change.

Instant gratification is not a realistic expectation, because many things in life are the result of a process, as we saw earlier. Expecting things quickly is normal and striving for efficiency is good—but don't forget about patience and perseverance.

Our Upbringing Is Different from Generations Past

In many cases, our upbringing varies from our parents and the generations before them. They did the "hard work" of starting businesses or building wealth from scratch, and because of their efforts, many young people are able to start a lot further ahead without the sacrifice or struggle that generations before them felt. As a result, older generations might feel that our generation is spoiled, or that we don't appreciate what we have and don't have a good work ethic.

It's important to note that this is *not* the experience of many people in our generation. Some of us grew up in comfortable middle-class or upper-class contexts and some of us did not. But for those who were raised in a more economically privileged home, it is important to appreciate that blessing. Regardless of how we were raised, it is important to realize that our generation has more access to education, resources, and technology than the generations before us.

We've Been Told We Can Do Anything

Since we were kids, we have been told that we can be anything we want and do anything we want. We can be the stars of our show. We can choose our destiny. The problem with this idea is that it's not totally true. I think we can all agree we can't just be or do anything we want. It's important to encourage kids, of course, and I'm glad I grew up hearing positive reinforcement. If you didn't grow up that way, I'm so sorry, because encouragement is truly valuable. But my point is that this be-anything-do-anything expectation can become unrealistic very quickly.

Many of us have chased larger-than-life dreams and set out to change the world in the process. Maybe at some point we even looked down on people who we perceived to be limited in their ambitions. Those who aspired to nothing more than a weekly paycheck or lived for the weekend. We saw their lives and swore we would be different. We promised ourselves we would do something that not only made us feel alive but also made an impact. But while chasing those admirable goals, somewhere along the way, we might have gotten a little tripped up in entitlement.

All three of these things—fast-paced lifestyles, present-day privilege, and encouragement—can be good, of course. Don't get me wrong. But the problem comes when we allow them to create expectations that are too narrow. By doing so, we can actually thwart our own dreams. That is, if we demand things too *quickly* or we expect them to be too *easy* or we only want to do *really awesome things,* we can become discouraged or disillusioned and will likely give up. Our generation's reputation is that when we don't see the results we want in our timing, we quit. We have huge dreams, but we won't see them come to pass if we lose hope in the process.

ALL ABOUT ME

I have some firsthand experience with entitlement, unfortunately. As I've mentioned, my parents are world-renowned authors and speakers. They always tried their best to remind their children how blessed we were to be able to travel across the country and be welcomed as guests in many different places. Sometimes they would sit my brothers and me down and remind us that speaking, writing, and traveling wasn't *their* ministry but *God's.* In their eyes, everything we'd been given was from God. Because they were humble and grateful for all of the opportunities God had given them, they didn't see the good things as a result of their efforts. They saw them as gifts of God's grace that needed to be used and administrated well.

That's a great attitude. There is nothing entitled about either of my parents' attitudes. And growing up, I didn't believe I had an entitlement problem either. I didn't care how nice the hotels we stayed in were. I wasn't picky about the food I ate. I was simply along for the ride. Although I saw the good fruit that humility produced in my parents, and although I didn't think I was entitled myself, I discovered later on that there are many ways entitlement can manifest itself in our lives, and some are very subtle.

Here's how I came to recognize my entitlement. After high school, I moved away from home to continue my education and to complete an internship program. When I moved back, I knew God had called me to work alongside my mom and dad, and I felt blessed to have that opportunity.

But I had high expectations, and they mostly started and ended with me. I had my *own* hopes and dreams for the future and many things I wanted to see fulfilled in my ministry. In fact, if those things *didn't* happen, I felt like I wouldn't make an impact on the world the way I was supposed to.

While God is the one who gives us dreams and desires, we have to be careful to guard our hearts in the process. In my mind, I was coming to my parents' ministry with a fresh perspective, and that meant I deserved a chance to create something new, something incredible, something that was my own. My thoughts were focused on *me* and what *I* deserved. And sadly, I had it all wrong.

During that season, I was miserable. Not because of the people working there or the job itself but because of my attitude. My own entitlement made me miserable!

Of course, I didn't see it that way at the time. I believed that since I had such big dreams, my parents needed to provide me with the steps to fulfill them. They were the bosses, after all! And they were the ones who had told my brothers and me since we were kids that we could accomplish more than they ever did. *They* encouraged the dreams and desires in me, and now *they* needed to make a way for them to happen.

I sat around waiting for opportunities to fall in my lap. The longer I waited, the more impatient I became. I was upset because I felt like I had more potential and that my gifts weren't being utilized. I thought, *I can do so much more, yet my parents are holding me back.*

Because my dreams and desires weren't being fulfilled, *I* felt unfulfilled. And I blamed my parents. I repeatedly told them that if they weren't going to do something about my lack of fulfillment, I was going to leave their ministry and become a youth pastor somewhere else.

I'm so glad I didn't follow through with that threat. To start with, I would have been a terrible youth pastor, because I clearly had some heart issues. If I was that bitter and angry working for my parents, imagine what a nightmare I would have been working for someone else.

Over time, I realized that the problem was *me*. It wasn't an immediate revelation but rather a result of maturity and perspective. To start with, I went back to school. Education expanded my knowledge and my experience, and it helped me see things from a less self-centered perspective. Maybe even more significantly, I began serving in a local church. The weekly opportunities to serve, along with the relationships I built and the mentoring I received, also improved my perspective. I guess I had to get outside my bubble to understand just how blessed I was. During that season, I grew to appreciate all of the work my parents were pouring into their ministry (correction: God's ministry), and I realized how entitled I'd been when I'd first started working for them.

When I moved back home a second time, I had a new outlook. I no longer expected my parents to help me fulfill my dreams, but instead I wanted to find ways I could serve theirs. Realizing how much they had done for me made me want to do more for them. I expressed my gratitude and told them about my desire to work for their ministry again.

But before I could come back, I needed to restore broken trust with a lot of my former coworkers. They saw an entitled, spoiled kid who wasn't grateful for the work he'd been given, and honestly, I didn't blame them. I had to own up to my mistakes, humble myself, and apologize for my immaturity.

So that's exactly what I did. I met with as many people as I could and asked for forgiveness. It wasn't easy, but it was a necessary step to earn their trust again. More than that, it was a stand against the impact of entitlement on my attitude and my actions.

Something shifted in my life in that season. I still had the same dreams and desires I had before, but my mindset was different. I no longer thought my parents or the ministry owed me anything. Instead, I focused my mental energy on things that could move the ministry forward. I was quick to ask my parents for their blessing on projects. If they didn't give it to me, I'd seek feedback on how I could grow or improve. My job was only part-time, and I made less money than I did before, but the truth is, I had never felt so grateful!

SPOILED ROYALS

Even though entitlement feels like a label that is uniquely targeted at our generation, it isn't a new condition and it certainly isn't something that impacts millennials only. The story of King Ahab in 1 Kings 21 is one of the best examples I know of someone with an entitled spirit.

As the king of Israel, Ahab could have had pretty much anything he wanted, whenever he wanted it. But one day, Ahab decided he wanted a particular vineyard that bordered his property. His plan was to use it as a vegetable garden. So he offered the owner of the vineyard, a man named Naboth, a large sum of money or a better vineyard in exchange.

Naboth declined both. The vineyard had been in his family for years, and he wasn't willing to sell his family inheritance.

Ahab was furious! He went back to his room, buried his face in his pillow, and refused to eat. It was a full-on royal temper tantrum.

I'm sure we've all had an Ahab moment like this. Maybe you realized in the middle of your anger that you were overreacting or that you were creating more of a problem by responding so childishly. But often it's more comfortable to harbor a negative attitude than to dig deep into our heart and find the real problem. In those moments, we need someone we can trust to get real with us and call us out on our juvenile behavior.

Unfortunately for Ahab, his wife, Jezebel, was not willing to do that.

Jezebel walked in on his tantrum, and instead of addressing the issue and challenging him to steer away from selfishness, Jezebel empowered his anger. Her language is the epitome of entitlement.

"Are you the king of Israel or not?" Jezebel demanded. "Get up and eat something, and don't worry about it. I'll get you Naboth's vineyard!" (1 Kings 21:7 NLT)

Jezebel came up with a plan. She wrote letters to the elders in Naboth's city, commanding them to falsely accuse Naboth of blaspheming God and the king, so that they would stone him to death as punishment. To make it official, she put the king's seal on all the letters, which implied that Ahab had written them.

The plan worked. Naboth lost his life because of the sense of entitlement that Ahab and Jezebel harbored. Jezebel reported the news to Ahab, and he immediately claimed the vineyard for himself. He finally had what he wanted.

This is an extreme example of how entitlement can harm us and others, of course. But it's exactly what many of us do, on a slightly less dramatic level, when we're under the influence of entitlement. I say influence because, just like alcohol, entitlement will impair our judgement and cause us to act out of character. We have been given much—but if we allow ourselves to become seduced by entitlement, we will care only about what we *don't* have, which will take us down a dark path.

When I look back at that season of harbored frustration while working in my parents' ministry, I recognize the attitude of Ahab. I wanted something that I believed would be beneficial for me. I felt like I deserved more, even if it meant stealing opportunities from others or demanding them prematurely. But that wasn't what God wanted. If I had gotten what I felt entitled to, it would have only offered me a momentary sense of happiness. Ultimately, it wouldn't have taken me where God wanted me to be, and it would have separated me further from his plan.

The attitude of entitlement didn't work out well for Ahab either. God sent the prophet Elijah to tell Ahab that he would die in the same place where Naboth was killed because he had stolen something that wasn't his and he had done so through violence (1 Kings 21:17–26). Again, you and I likely won't face consequences this severe, but we will reap what we sow. Entitlement will keep us from God's calling, but humility, patience, and gratitude will take us toward it.

GOD'S GOT YOU COVERED

As we've seen already, God didn't design us to be entitled but to be grateful. The two are mutually exclusive. Entitlement focuses on self—on what we want, demand, and deserve. It is never satisfied, because no amount of self-gratification can bring true satisfaction.

Gratitude, on the other hand, focuses on others—on their value, their contributions, and their importance. It includes satisfaction in its very definition, and therefore it has the power to bring inner peace and contentment. Before we seek the things we are dreaming of or believe are ours, we must choose to start with thankfulness.

When I began working for my parents, I lacked gratitude, and I also lacked patience. The two are often connected. Gratitude fosters patience because it keeps our hearts in a place of satisfaction rather than restlessness. In my case, I couldn't see what I had to be thankful for, so I became impatient to receive what I envisioned as *my* right and *my* future.

This focus on my rights and my future highlights what impatience and entitlement have in common: an absorption with self. The problem isn't with our rights and dreams, because those things very likely are in God's heart as well. The problem is that we focus so exclusively, and so obsessively, on *us*.

We need to know something though. God cares about our rights, our dreams, our desires, and our goals. We don't have to obsess over getting them for ourselves, because we can trust him to fulfill his plans for us.

During that season, I remember listening to a preacher talk about welcoming his first daughter into the world. One statement he made will stay with me forever. He said that when he looked into her eyes, he realized that the greatest thing he could do with his life was raise that child. He didn't know what her dreams and desires would be, but he knew that whatever they were, he'd do everything in his power to fulfill them. Why? Because he was absolutely in love with his child. Then he shared this revelation. Because we are children of God, God looks at us the same way.

Think about that for a second. We are all God's creation. He has placed dreams and desires in our hearts, and he wants to see them fulfilled even more than we do. If we can embrace our identity as children of God, we will overcome our urge to gain things on our own. We will rest in the fact that we have a God who is for us and wants to see good things fulfilled in our lives. We will trust his timing, not ours. Instead of striving, we will be patient. Instead of feeling entitled, we will be grateful.

We must shift our focus away from what we think we deserve or need and put it on the things God has so graciously given us.

The idea of resting our dreams on God doesn't refer to laziness or inactivity, of course. God puts dreams and desires in our heart, and he wants us to pursue them. He wants us to dream big, to be excited about the future, and to chase after what we want. But our work and our efforts should be birthed from gratitude, not from human striving. They should be the natural result of hearts that are secure in God's love and patient in his process.

Gratitude—accompanied with patience—is our generation's secret weapon in the battle to eliminate our sense of entitlement.

Sometimes the distance between where we are and where we want to be is great. It takes great patience to keep us going while we're waiting in the gap. But when we're patient, we leave room for God's timing.

As I write this chapter, years after first working for my parents, God has allowed me to see many of those dreams I had as a teenager grow into reality. And he's continued to place bigger and wilder dreams in my heart. Two years after I returned to the ministry, I cofounded a ministry for youth and young adults called Sons and Daughters, along with my siblings. To me, it's a visible reminder of the work God has done in my character.

In hindsight, I can see that God's timing was not only worth the wait but it made all the difference in what those dreams would become. I've realized the things I had in my heart were far bigger than me. They required the contribution of many people working together without selfish ambition or self-focused dreams. Today, Sons and Daughters is equipping a generation of leaders all around the world, and my heart is full of gratitude for the work that's being done.

I believe we are a generation of world changers. We are eager to leave our communities, our nation, and our world better than we found them. That requires thinking big, taking risks, working hard, and not settling for the mundane. But it also takes patience, humility, and ongoing gratitude.

As we seek the adventure ahead of us, we can take heart in knowing that God will see us through. May our generation leave a mark—not as entitled, hard-to-employ millennials but as thankful, hardworking movers and shakers!

WE ARE A GRATEFUL GENERATION,

NOT AN ENTITLED GENERATION.

WE KNOW GOD HAS CALLED US

AND THE WORLD NEEDS US.

WE ARE PATIENT IN THE PROCESS

AND COMMITTED TO THE FUTURE.

ELEVEN

What comes into our minds when we think about God is the most important thing about us.

A. W. Tozer

THERE IS A FEAR that makes us fearless. It's a fear that restrains us and yet also empowers us. A fear that enables us to stand, to fight, and to win.

You might be a bit confused right now, because most of us have been taught that fear is unhealthy. But I'm not talking about the negative fears which are unfortunately so common in our generation: fear of failure, fear of the future, fear of missing out. Our generation has become fearful in all the wrong ways about all the wrong things.

No, the fear I'm talking about makes us stand out from the crowd. It keeps us from being deceived by wrong thinking or harmful pursuits. It causes us to seek wisdom, and it prompts us to stand in awe of our creator.

It's a fear that causes us to live fearlessly. It's called the fear of God. In the book of Proverbs, Solomon tells us that the fear of the Lord is the beginning of wisdom and knowledge (1:7; 9:10). He said it prolongs life (10:27), gives us strong confidence (14:26), is a fountain of life (14:27), keeps us from evil (16:6), and leads to riches, honor, and life (22:4). With a résumé like that, we should probably take this concept seriously. And yet, many of us likely don't really know what it means to fear the Lord.

ALL OF GOD

Before we dive more into what this fear looks like, though, there's something I want to make sure you understand. God is a God of relationship, and he wants a relationship with you. Do you know how amazing that is? I stand in awe of the fact that God would create us with relationship in mind. He is our Father, our Lord, and our King, and he wants to be close to us.

Sometimes we use those titles without really thinking about the magnitude of what they mean. We see him as the Father who loves us and sent his Son to die on the cross for us. That concept is so important to understand and embrace—but it's just one facet of who God is. We call him Lord in our prayers, but do we actually give him dominion over our lives? We say he is the King of Kings, but do we stand in awe of his power and sovereignty?

These titles matter because in order to have a relationship with God, we must acknowledge who he is. Not just part of who he is and not just some of what he's done but *all* of it. We must comprehend, as much as humanly possible, the full nature of God. That means knowing his love but also knowing his power. It means knowing his mercy but also knowing his holiness.

None of those things are at odds with each other either. God is not schizophrenic or manic-depressive. He is always the same, but he is so much bigger than just a single facet. If we were to reduce him to love or to wisdom or to peace or to power or to any other single attribute, we would be missing out on the vastness of God.

If our mindset about God is limited, our ability to relate to him will be as well. Just as a friendship gets richer the more we know about each other, and just as a marriage becomes more beautiful as both spouses understand and trust each other more, so our walk with God improves as we gain a deeper understanding of him.

That is why the fear of God is actually incredibly healthy and liberating for our walk with him. We'll discuss this more in a moment, but the Bible clearly encourages us to fear God. I mentioned a few of those references in Proverbs, but look at these words from Psalm 89:7.

> God is greatly to be feared in the assembly of the
> saints,
> And to be held in reverence by all those around Him.
> (NKJV)

I've encountered people who don't like verses like this. And I get it—the Bible seems to present contrasting ideas about fear. For example, I've heard people quote the following verse and say that there is no room for fear in a relationship with God.

There is no fear in love. But perfect love drives out fear, because fear has to do with punishment. The one who fears is
not made perfect in love. (1 John 4:18)

So, which is it? Should we fear or love or both? Does love
cast out fear or can we fear God and love him at the same
time? And if fear and love can coexist, what effect will that
have on our relationship with God? To address these questions, we need to understand more about the fear of God.

TWO KINDS OF FEAR

To begin, it's imperative to realize there are two different
types of fear in the Bible. The fear of God is *not* the same
kind of fear as a fear of the dark, for example, or a fear of
death.

Exodus 20:20 addresses both kinds of fear.

Moses said to the people, "Do not *fear*; for God has come
to test you, and that His *fear* may be before you, so that you
may not sin." (NKJV, my emphasis)

At face value, this is an extremely confusing verse: Don't
fear! Why? Because God is coming so that you'll have fear!
What?

Clarity comes when you realize there are two kinds of
fear represented here. The first is the standard definition of
fear. It's a negative term that means being terrified. Moses
told the people *not* to have this fear, because it wasn't doing
them any good. God didn't want them to dread him or to be
afraid he was going to zap them with lightning any second.

The second type of fear, though, is one we need more of—the fear of God. Moses told the people that God was going to reveal himself to them so that they would know who he is—his power, his greatness, his holiness, and his love. Moses didn't want them to underestimate God or to take him for granted. They needed to see him as more than a legend or a distant cloud. He is God, the king of the universe, the creator of all, the ever-present Lord, the ultimate authority, the Father and King.

Full knowledge of God is described as *fear*. You could use words like *awe* or *awestruck* as well. The emphasis is not on shaking in our boots but on bowing our knees. It's not on running away in terror but on drawing close in respect. It's about knowing God and maintaining a healthy relationship with him.

Fearing God doesn't mean being afraid of God. When I was a kid, I remember feeling like I needed to give my life to Christ each week because I was scared of God. I thought he was standing over me, ready to hit me with a hammer if I didn't confess my sins and repent. I didn't understand the completeness of salvation, so I lived terrified that I was going to hell if I didn't get re-saved on a regular basis.

That definitely was not healthy fear! It was based on an inaccurate perception of God. I was only seeing one facet of God, and not even an accurate one at that. I only viewed God as a judge who would punish me. I didn't have a genuine fear of God, but actually the opposite. I had a limited, low view of God that produced unhealthy anxiety.

I love this quote by A. W Tozer: "A low view of God is the cause of a hundred lesser evils. A high view of God is the solution to ten thousand temporal problems."[1]

A "low view" of God is an understanding based on limited knowledge, and it produces wrong fear and ultimately wrong actions. A "high view" is based on full knowledge and revelation; it is a healthy fear that keeps us safe and correctly aligned with God.

MY FEARS

I've seen unhealthy fear play out in my life in other ways too. One of those is what the Bible calls the "fear of man," and it is one of the most common fears we face. It means being afraid of what other people think, say, or do.

> Fear of man will prove to be a snare,
> but whoever trusts in the LORD is kept safe. (Prov. 29:25)

When I was younger, I was afraid to talk about Jesus or tell people I was a Christian. I was constantly worried what people would think of me if they knew I was a believer.

Of course, I came from a family whose entire purpose revolved around Jesus, so it was hard to hide! When someone would ask me what my parents did for a living, I would freeze up. I would tell people my parents were authors in an effort to keep things as vague as possible. Then they would ask me what books they had written. Being the resourceful kid I was, I would give them the book titles that sounded nonreligious. I would avoid ones like *The Bait of Satan, Thus Saith The Lord,* and, of course, *The Devil's Door!*

Looking back, I don't blame myself for omitting some of those titles. They're intense, right? But my strategy wasn't foolproof. Often I'd be asked what my parents' books were about. At that point, I'd be sweating. My typical response would be something like, "Oh, you know, just how to live well . . . and stuff."

By then, most people would start to pick up on the fact that my parents wrote books on Christianity and faith, and I'd be cornered.

I was so scared of what people would think of me because I was afraid I'd be rejected or judged or held to a higher standard. I allowed this fear to control the opportunities to share the gospel with people in what would have been a completely natural way.

Then one day, something happened. I was at a Bible study at my friend's house, and the leader asked us to find a quiet place to spend time with God. I remember sitting in silence for some time, not knowing what to do, just asking God to speak to me.

I decided to open my Bible, and I found myself in Matthew 13. The story recounts how a farmer scatters seed all over but only a few of the seeds actually take root and grow. I remember God speaking so clearly to me: *This is what I want you to do. Go scatter seed in your school. Go tell people about me.*

I remember the moment as if it were yesterday. The fire of God seemed so evident in my life that night, and I was excited to go into my school with this newfound purpose and plan.

But then the next day came, and the reality of what I was supposed to do hit me. Fear began to creep in. And to my shame, I have to say that I went back to the same life I was living before. I didn't share the gospel with those around me until long after that day. I even had friends ask me about Christianity, and I would downplay my faith because I cared more about their opinion of me than their salvation.

I feared the opinions of others more than I feared God.

Fear is serious. That's why it's so important to avoid the wrong kind of fear and have the right view of God. God wants us to know that we must take him seriously. Calling him Lord and King cannot be a flippant thing that we take lightly.

Actually, all fear bends our will, including the negative kinds of fear. For example, if you have a fear of talking to new people, you will subconsciously—and sometimes consciously—avoid situations where you would meet new people. You have bent to the will of that master.

When you fear the Lord, you bend your life to God's will— even when it's beyond your current comprehension.

Unlike the wrong fear, which the enemy uses to steal, kill, and destroy, the fear of the Lord draws you closer to the heart of the Father and opens your eyes to his plans for your life.

Eventually, my relationship with God conquered that unhealthy fear of others' opinions, and I was able to share my faith. I was able to take a look at the root of that fear, address it, and change my mindset toward it. Ironically, what was once my greatest fear is now what I base my life around! Do I still get a little nervous when I share Jesus with someone? Honestly, yes. But that fear no longer controls me. Instead, my knowledge of God and my relationship with him determine my actions.

WORST-CASE SCENARIO

The wrong kind of fear has power, but it's a power based on an expected or assumed reality. In other words, we feel afraid of what might happen or will probably happen before it happens. As humans, we have great imaginations, so fear has a lot of material to work with. But our imaginations can actually work for us if we are intentional about facing our fears rather than running from them.

Let me illustrate with a story. One morning, before leaving for work, I went downstairs to make breakfast. I took out the blender and walked toward the refrigerator. In the process, I stepped on something that felt like a small rope. I didn't react very quickly since I was still half asleep. But then I wondered, *What was that?* I looked down and saw a snake coming straight for me! He was genuinely mad that I had the nerve to step on him in my own house.

For context, let me say that I am not the guy you call when you see a snake. Anyone close to me knows that. This was literally my greatest nightmare coming true.

I started yelling. And it wasn't a manly yell; it was more like a terrified scream. I woke up the entire family with my reaction. The snake didn't even have teeth and he was the size of one of my fingers, yet there I was, a 6'2", two-hundred-pound guy, standing on the counter and yelling for help.

For me, this was the worst-case scenario. What I had always feared had materialized before my eyes. And . . . nothing happened. My family rescued me, the snake retreated, and I climbed down from the counter, slightly embarrassed but mostly relieved.

Snakes are one of my real fears. Yet when the supposed

worst-case scenario happened—stepping on a snake in my own kitchen—it wasn't nearly as big of a deal as I feared it would be. Remember, fear's power is based in the possibility of something rather than the reality of that thing. It's in the maybes, the mights, and the probablies.

Yes, some fears are understandable, but they shouldn't immobilize us. And we must never let unhealthy fear dictate our lives.

I've heard fear defined this way: False Evidence Appearing Real. In other words, it's a mirage, a hologram, something projected into reality that probably won't even happen. And even if it does, it won't be as terrifying as we think.

My fear of sharing my faith was exactly that: a false belief. I let the worst-case scenarios of rejection and mocking silence me, and they hadn't even happened!

What I've found useful in navigating fear is a fairly simple process:

Acknowledge the fear → Identify the worst-case scenario → Accept it → Move forward

Pause for a second to think about your own life. What fear has been holding you back from living? From truly living up to your potential?

The fear of failure?

The fear of rejection?

The fear of being alone?

The fear of financial loss?

The fear of illness or death?

The fear of being controlled?

The fear of being laughed at?

The fear of being insignificant?

The first step in defeating your fear is acknowledging and

naming it. These are far stronger fears than a fear of snakes, by the way. They have the power to limit your dreams and interrupt your calling. But when you identify fear and recognize it for what it is—a lie, a supposition, an assumption—it loses much of its power.

Once you've identified the fear, ask yourself this: *What is the worst-case scenario regarding this fear?* Is it that you will stay in the same job the rest of your life? That you might experience some discomfort or awkwardness? That someone will walk out of your life and potentially not return?

Write down your responses. Just seeing them in writing will reduce the power that fear has over you. Come back to those words when you're struggling with that fear. Because unless your worst-case scenario is "The world will cease to exist," you can accept your fear for what it is and move forward.

THE GOOD FEAR

Let's return to the idea of healthy fear, which is the fear of God. As I mentioned earlier, this is the fear that will allow you to live in the fullness of God's calling for your life.

I believe it takes two things to be successful in life. One, you must remain teachable, which means you never feel like you can stop growing because you've "made it." And two, you must have a healthy fear of God. The two are connected, actually.

When God gave Solomon the choice to have anything he wanted, he responded by requesting the ability to tell the difference between right and wrong. He longed for wisdom to know how to make good decisions and lead well (2 Chron.

1:10). Don't we all wish we had that? The amazing thing is that we *can*. As I mentioned above, Solomon told us that the beginning of wisdom is the fear of the Lord. That fear gives us the ability to tell the difference between right and wrong. It gives us discernment, it helps us make wise decisions, and it guides our lives in every area.

As pastor Andy Stanley points out in his book *Ask It*, Psalms and Proverbs talk about four different kinds of people: the fool, the mocker, the simple, and the wise. (For examples of each, look at Proverbs 18:2–3, Psalms 14:1–2, and 119:130). When listening to correction or instruction, each of these kinds of people will respond differently.

The fool will ignore correction.

The mocker will hate it.

The simple just won't get it.

The wise person will appreciate it.[2]

The difference between these four comes down to application. The fool, the mocker, and the simple will respond with a self-focused fear. They will be deterred by the pain, the shame, the work, and the humility required to implement change. But the wise will respond with godly fear, and they will apply the correction that's been given to their life.

The connection between fearing God and living wisely is really a question of applying the truths we have learned from God to our lives. Notice God's blessing in Deuteronomy 5:29: "Oh, that their hearts would be inclined to fear me and keep all my commands always, so that it might go well with them and their children forever!"

Our fear of God causes us to honor his Word, and when we honor his Word, we are successful.

Consider Abraham. God told him to sacrifice Isaac, the son God had promised him. Most of us would probably argue with God in this situation. But we see the immediate obedience of Abraham recorded in the Bible. Early the next morning he rose and began his journey. Before he completed the sacrifice, though, an angel of the Lord stopped him and said, "Now I know that you fear God" (Gen. 22:12).

Abraham's fear of God prompted his obedience, even when the command didn't make sense. He knew God well enough and trusted him deeply enough to obey him no matter what he asked. The author of Hebrews mentions that Abraham "reasoned that if Isaac died, God was able to bring him back to life again" (11:19 NLT). That was how deeply Abraham honored and believed in God. No wonder Abraham is called the father of all who believe!

I love this quote by theologian Timothy Keller: "If your god never disagrees with you, you might just be worshiping an idealized version of yourself."[3]

Abraham must have been confused by God's commands, but he was willing to submit his will and actions to him. In the same way, we need to make sure we are listening to God, understanding his will, and letting our lives be guided by him. A healthy fear of God will do exactly that: remind us to take the commands of God seriously.

As we look through Scripture, there are countless examples of how fearing God and honoring his commands benefit us.

- Joseph won favor from his brothers because he was a God-fearing man. (Gen. 42:18)

- Because the midwives feared God, they spared the Hebrew babies, saving Moses's life. (Exod. 1:17)
- When Moses chose new leaders to help him, a key requirement was that they feared God. (Exod. 18:21)

It's not just an Old Testament principle either.

- Jesus tells us not to fear men, who can only affect our earthly bodies, but rather to fear God, because he determines our eternal destiny. (Matt. 10:28)
- Paul told the Corinthians to work toward complete holiness in the fear of God. (2 Cor. 7:1)
- The early church grew and thrived in the fear of the Lord. (Acts 9:31)[4]

And to top it all off, there is an interesting passage in Romans 3 that describes the sinful, destructive lifestyle of those who don't follow God. The passage sums up this attitude by saying there is no fear of God in the life of those who don't follow God's commands (v. 18).

We can't fear the world or bend to its will. Instead, we need the fear of God, the fear that makes us fearless. I love the way writer William D. Eisenhower put it in his article "Fearing God":

Unfortunately, many of us presume that the world is the ultimate threat and that God's function is to offset it. How different this is from the biblical position that God is far scarier than the world. . . . When we assume that the world is the ultimate threat, we give it unwarranted power, for in truth, the world's threats are temporary. When we expect God to balance the stress of the world, we reduce him to the world's equal. . . . As I walk with the Lord, I discover that God poses an ominous threat to my ego, but not to me. He rescues me from my delusions, so he may reveal the truth that sets me free. He casts me down, only to lift me up again. He sits in judgment of my sin, but forgives me, nevertheless. Fear of the Lord is the beginning of wisdom, but love from the Lord is its completion.[5]

When we look at the amazing display of love God extended toward us by sending Jesus, what is left to fear in this world other than God?

In summary, let me give you three simple practices to develop and live with a healthy fear of the Lord.

1. **Acknowledge him.** Recognize who God is. He is holy, he is perfect, he is king. He deserves your complete loyalty and trust.
2. **Be in awe of him.** Look at the incredible things that God has done in your life and be amazed by his power, his goodness, and his presence.
3. **Yield to him.** When you see something one way and God sees it another, he's right. God gets the last word. It's more than just repeating "Your will be done, not mine"; it's reflecting that humility and submission in your lifestyle.

FRIENDS OF GOD

As we conclude this chapter, remember that the fear of the Lord strengthens our friendship with God. King David wrote this in the book of Psalms: "The LORD confides in those who fear him; he makes his covenant known to them" (25:14).

Can you imagine being the person God shares his secrets with? I can hardly begin to fathom this, which is why I always want to fear God.

As I mentioned in an earlier chapter, my dad always says that the fear of God is not about being *afraid* of God; it's about being afraid of being *away* from him. It's the fear of drifting from his commandments. It's the fear of having your life be dictated by anything other than God.

This is God's calling over our generation. That we would be a generation that lives fearlessly as friends with God not a generation that lives fearfully. That we would fear God so much that he could share his secrets with us. That no matter how crazy the world gets or how much madness seems to be playing out in front of our eyes, we would boldly stick to what the word of God says because he is the only thing that captivates our attention.

In closing, I want to leave you with this Scripture.

> The fear of the LORD is pure,
>   enduring forever.
> The decrees of the LORD are firm,
>   and all of them are righteous.
>
> They are more precious than gold,
>   than much pure gold;
> they are sweeter than honey,
>   than honey from the honeycomb.
> By them your servant is warned;
>   in keeping them there is great reward. (Ps. 19:9–14)

When we learn to fear God, we are able to live fearlessly. Let's allow our knowledge of God and our awe of him to embolden us as we live out our calling in him!

WE ARE A GENERATION WHO **FEARS GOD—**

NOTHING ELSE AND NO ONE ELSE.

WE KNOW HIM, LOVE HIM, AND TRUST HIM.

AND WE STAND IN AWE OF HIM.

TWELVE

THE POWER OF A THOUGHT

> But if thought corrupts language, language can also corrupt thought.
>
> George Orwell

THROUGHOUT THIS BOOK, we've talked about the power of a spoken word and how it can shape our reality. Words form our identity. They mold our future. We've looked at ten negative labels that we often hear and believe about ourselves, and we've uncovered the godly truths that overcome the negativity and shine light on our God-given calling.

I want to end our time together talking about the power of a thought.

Every word we speak originates as a thought. We give credit to our tongue for pronouncing the words we speak, but we don't give enough credit to our minds for conceiving those words. Whether conscious or subconscious, our words, phrases, and sentences flow from the ideas inside our heads. That is why it is so important to control what we think.

Even the field of science recognizes the power of thought, and medical studies have shown that what people believe can impact the way their bodies respond to treatment. For example, consider the placebo effect, which is a scientific term for the phenomenon that occurs when someone feels better after taking a medicine that could not have produced the result. In other words, their belief influences their improvement, not the actual medicine.

In many studies, researchers must take the placebo effect into account for their control group. Otherwise, the psychological effect of taking a pill (or not taking a pill) can blur the results. So they'll give one group of participants the medicine they are testing, and they'll give the control group sugar pills made to resemble medicine. But as far as the participants know, they are all receiving genuine medication. They all expect results, and often they all see results, even though what some of them swallowed was a few extra grams of sugar.

The sugar pills often work because the patients expect their bodies to get better. And they do! Obviously that only works to a point—but it's a fascinating point. The mind achieves what it believes.

I've heard it said that when you change your mind, it will change your reality. One of my favorite quotes, typically attributed to Dr. Wayne Dyer, puts it this way: "Change the way you look at things, and the things you look at change."[1]

THE POWER TO THINK

In the first chapter, we talked about living according to God's design and calling instead of basing our actions on negative labels. We saw that in order to build a life-giving environment, we need to reshape our words and base them on God's truth instead of the opinions of the world. God has given us the ability to think, and those thoughts have power to shape everything around us.

Our future starts with a thought. It begins with an intentional choice to say, "I'm not going to believe the negative things spoken over me. Instead, I'm going to believe only what God says about me. I'm going to focus on things that line up with what is true."

Jesus put it this way: "For whatever is in your heart determines what you say" (Matt. 12:34 NLT).

It isn't what we say or do that controls us; it is our hearts that control us. Our words simply reflect our hearts. So as we think about how we want to be defined and how we want to live, we need to make sure our thoughts are intentionally leading us in that direction.

No circumstance or situation can directly create a certain emotion. No situation by itself can create fear, discouragement, loneliness, doubt, or regret. It is our subconscious response to circumstances that produces these negative feelings. Our thoughts about a situation will ultimately shape our view of it.

In fact, everything we allow into our lives shapes our subconscious. Never before has a generation been so exposed or had so much access to so much visual, auditory, and written content. Unfortunately, that content also promotes destructive things like violence, drugs, pornography, fear, and profanity. And the more we're exposed to these things, the more likely it is that our subconscious will take hold of them.

When I was younger, I listened to some pretty unhealthy music. My parents would discipline me if they caught me listening to it. I would argue with them, saying things like, "I'm not even paying attention to the lyrics, I just like the beat." And my mom would remind me of how powerful words are. She'd tell me that the more I listened to those songs, the more those lyrics would get into my heart and change my thinking without me even realizing it.

At the time, I brushed off her warnings. But later, I found out it was true. The lyrics talked about things like drugs, alcohol, and illicit sex. I knew those pursuits had the potential to be destructive, but the songs began to normalize them for me. Over time, my attitude toward those things became more casual. I started drinking. I became addicted to porn. I dated a girl who wasn't a Christian, and I compromised some of my values with her. The things I once knew to be dangerous seemed normal.

Thankfully, I didn't stay on that path. My trajectory changed when I later came back to God. But coming back meant I also needed to start being more intentional about what I allowed to influence my mind.

I'm not saying that all secular music is bad or from the devil and I'm not saying that listening to it will cause you to start doing drugs and hooking up with random people. I'm simply saying that we have to be careful about what we allow into our subconscious. Our thoughts are powerful, and we have to guard them.

Studies show that we only make 4 to 6 percent of our decisions consciously. The rest are made instantly through our subconscious. It's interesting that about 95 percent of our decisions are made without intentional thought.[2]

In a way, you and I are only exercising our free will 4 to 6 percent of the time. Think about that. Our free will—the thing God gave us to choose him—is rarely in charge! Our subconscious, which is formed by the things we take in all the time—words, movies, music, images, and so on—is primarily in charge, whether we are aware of it or not.

When we normalize things in our mind, our subconscious leans into them. Sadly, that's often how addictions are formed, as we discussed earlier. Over time, our subconscious leads us to believe that our behavior is normal and good. Then, when the opportunity arises for us to act out, it becomes incredibly difficult to say no. Why? Because our subconscious is not based on rationality but on repetition. What we are exposed to over and over becomes our version of "normal."

Paul said it this way in Romans: "Do not conform to the pattern of this world, but be transformed by the renewing of the mind" (12:2).

If you want to see your life changed, you have to start by filtering the things that come in contact with your mind. Invite God into every part of your thinking. Let him take your thoughts captive and lead you in the right direction.

It's not enough to just *choose* the path of life; we have to also *stay* on it. After years of thinking one way, we will subconsciously want to continue down the path of least resistance, the path that was leading us to labels. But as we continually rewire our thoughts and redefine our lives, we'll begin to think and look more like God. Developing new ways of thinking and forming new neural pathways is like clearing a new path through a jungle—but once the paths are formed, our minds will naturally follow the new routes.

There is an old Cherokee legend about a grandfather who is talking to his grandson about life. He explains that inside everyone, there is a fight going on between two wolves. One wolf is evil: he is anger, envy, fear, and pride. The other wolf is good: he is compassion, faithfulness, love, and kindness. The boy thinks about the two wolves for a minute, then asks: "Which wolf will win the fight?" The grandfather replies, "Whichever one you feed."[3]

We can determine our thoughts and feelings by "feeding the good wolf" and being cautious about what we let influence our mind. Every day, somewhere between fifty thousand to seventy thousand thoughts pass through our brains. With a number that high, negative thoughts *will* be in the mix. But we get to control how much power we give those thoughts. We decide which thoughts to feed into our souls and which ones to reject.

The enemy constantly gives us wrong options: things that contradict God's calling for us or tempt us to believe that his promises aren't for us. My mom used to remind my brothers and me that the enemy comes to steal, kill, and destroy. He is a liar who only wants to take from us. He wants to whisper words of discouragement, destruction, and disbelief into our minds and negatively shape the way we think about God and ourselves.

That's why we must feed ourselves the right thoughts, the right words, and the right identity.

THE POWER TO CHOOSE

Not only has God given us the power to think but he has also given us the power to choose. We choose our thoughts, we choose how we see ourselves, and we choose the path we take in life.

There is a conversation between *Star Trek*'s iconic Spock and his father, Sarek, that highlights the power of choice. (And no, *Star Trek* can't compare to the Bible—but you can find inspiration anywhere!) As the child of an alien father and a human mother, Spock is trying to decide which identity and culture to embrace. Sarek says, "You are fully capable of deciding your own destiny. The question you face is, which path will you choose? This is something only you can decide."[4]

The setting is fictional, of course, but the declaration rings true for all of us as sons and daughters. We are fully capable of deciding our own destiny. We have the power to choose our journey. Jesus set before us the way of life or death, light or darkness, salvation or condemnation. It's up to us to decide which path we will choose.

Let me say it again. *We* have the power. *We* get to choose. Not because we know best but because God wants us to choose him. And when we choose him, we are choosing life.

God made it clear that we can only follow one way. We can't choose both. We can't stay in the middle. The world doesn't need a generation that tries to play both sides. It needs to see a generation filled with the incredible power that comes from understanding who we are in Christ. We need to be believers who actively choose life, who walk in the light, who have decided once and for all to make Jesus our Lord and Savior.

The thoughts you hold on to will influence your actions. They'll cause you to run *toward* something or *away* from it. I don't know about you, but I want to be influenced to run toward the life God has called me to. To do that, I must hold on to God's promises in my mind.

The same is true for all of us. We must be drawn toward God's words and let his thoughts speak louder than any others. It's time for us to speak truth over ourselves that aligns with God's Word.

- We are not lost; we are *focused* and found, chosen, and cherished by God.
- We are not broken; we are *restored* for God's purpose.
- We are not doubtful; we are *seeking* truth and finding answers.
- We are not regretful; we are *awakened* to our needs and our future.
- We are not offended; we are *blessed,* and we live in forgiveness and grace.
- We are not lacking; we are *made complete* by God with everything we need.
- We are not addicted; we are *fighting* for freedom in Christ.
- We are not discouraged; we are *hopeful* about God's plan for our lives.
- We are not entitled; we are *grateful* for all we have received.
- We are not fearful; we are *God-fearing,* and we live in intimate closeness with him.

When we feed ourselves God's truth, his words direct our thoughts, and our lives change as a result.

THE POWER TO CHANGE

Once we understand our power to think and our power to choose, we discover our power to change. We can change ourselves, we can change our generation, and we can change the world.

When we look at the world around us, it's not hard to see all that is going wrong. There are diseases that can't be cured, divorce is commonplace, anxiety is skyrocketing, and anger is taking over our social media feeds. At first glance, things are grim.

What gives me hope, however, is my belief that we can be the generation that changes things. We can be the generation that cures diseases, that solidifies marriages and families, that pursues peace, that speaks truth with love and kindness.

If we focus on what is true about us, we have the potential to change the world.

A couple of years ago, I started my new year off by praying for the months ahead. Normally I would have prayed for something tangible or visible, such as money or resources to do God's will. But not this time. I simply asked him for a thought. I wrote down, "God, please give me an idea." Why? Because when God gives us ideas, he is giving us the keys to the future. His grace will accompany us and his resources will sustain us but it must start with an idea.

Ask God to give you thoughts from him. Begin to speak words over yourself that support who he says you are and replace the limiting labels that have been spoken over you.

My prayer is that we will not be a generation defined by past labels but by God's calling to bring hope, healing, and change wherever we go. We will be a generation redefined by who God says we are. We will take hold of all that he has for us. We will step into our inheritance as sons and daughters of God. We will be a voice for the people around us. We'll be a generation that goes further than any before us because we're fully immersed in the knowledge of God and committed to the journey ahead.

Our world needs us. If we step into who we are in Jesus, the world will see his nature revealed through us. We are the light of the world, and it's time for us to embrace that calling. May we be a generation that's known for signs and wonders, justice and mercy, truth and grace, and adventure and fearlessness.

May we be known as sons and daughters of God.

ACKNOWLEDGMENTS

To my beautiful wife, Christian. Without you this book would have never been. You pushed me and challenged me to do something that I never believed to be possible. I love you.

To my parents, John and Lisa. You were the first to call out my true identity. I am the man I am today because of you.

To my brothers, Addison, Austin, and Alec. Thank you for always being there for me and pushing me to be the best man that I can be.

To my amazing editor, Jen. Thank you for believing in me and this book from the beginning.

Thank you to the Baker team for all your hard work and dedication to this project. I am truly honored to work with you.

NOTES

Chapter 1 The Power of a Word

1. Nickee De Leon Huld, "How Many Words Does the Average Person Know?" *Word Counter* (blog), accessed August 10, 2020, https://wordcounter.io/blog/how-many-words-does-the-average-person-know/.

Chapter 2 Lost

1. "Babel," *Lexico US Dictionary* (powered by Oxford, 2020), accessed August 10, 2020, https://www.lexico.com/en/definition/babel.

Chapter 3 Broken

1. Kelly Richman-Abdou, "Kintsugi: The Centuries-Old Art of Repairing Broken Pottery with Gold," My Modern Met, September 5, 2019, https://mymodernmet.com/kintsugi-kintsukuroi/.

Chapter 4 Doubtful

1. Definitions summarized from the *Bible Sense Lexicon*, Logos Bible Software (Faithlife Corporation: dataset 20 February 2020).
2. Read Thomas's full story in John 20:24–29.
3. Gary R. Habermas, "How Should a Christian Deal with Doubt?" *CSB Apologetics Study Bible* (Nashville: B&H, 2017), 1341.
4. Charles Spurgeon, *Spurgeon's Sermons Volume 1: 1855*, ed. Anthony Uyl (Woodstock, Ontario: Devoted Publishing, 2017), 200.
5. Read God's response to Job in Job 38–41.
6. Hillsong Music, "As It Is in Heaven," Let There Be Light, Hillsong, Sparrow, Capitol, 2016.

Chapter 5 Regretful

1. Read about David's mourning process in 2 Samuel 12:16–23.
2. Lucy Locket, "Tiger Woods' Mental Tricks," Golf a Lot, April 24, 2014, https://www.golfalot.com/instruction/tiger-woods-mental-tricks-2843.aspx.
3. "Atsab," BibleStudyTools, accessed August 10, 2020, https://www.biblestudytools.com/lexicons/hebrew/nas/atsab.html. Public domain.

Chapter 6 Offended

1. John Bevere, *The Bait of Satan* (Lake Mary, FL: Charisma House, 1984), 134.
2. Read the story of Saul's chase in 1 Samuel 24.

Chapter 8 Addicted

1. *Merriam-Webster.com Dictionary*, s.v. "addicted," accessed March 26, 2020, https://www.merriam-webster.com/dictionary/addicted.
2. Terry Cu-Unjieng, "Why 68% of Christian Men Watch Porn," The Conquer Series, https://conquerseries.com/why-68-percent-of-christian-men-watch-porn/.
3. Kimberly Perry, "What's the Average Age Kids See Internet Pornography? (Quite Young)," We Stand Guard, October 17, 2019, https://www.westandguard.com/what-s-the-average-age-kids-see-internet-pornography-quite-young.
4. "Millennials and Technology at Home," Qualtrics, accessed July 17, 2020, https://www.qualtrics.com/millennials/ebooks/Millennials_And_Tech_At_Home_eBook_All_AK.pdf.
5. "Time Flies: U.S. Adults Now Spend Nearly Half a Day Interacting with Media," Neilsen, July 31, 2018, https://www.nielsen.com/us/en/insights/article/2018/time-flies-us-adults-now-spend-nearly-half-a-day-interacting-with-media/.
6. John Bevere (@johnbevere), Twitter post, July 8, 2017, 10:02 a.m., https://twitter.com/JohnBevere/status/883687631023943680.
7. Ira Berkow, "Louis Zamperini, Olympian and 'Unbroken' War Survivor, Dies at 97," *New York Times*, July 3, 2014, https://www.nytimes.com/2014/07/04/arts/louis-zamperini-olympian-war-survivor-unbroken-dies.html.
8. Louis Zamperini, *Devil at My Heels: A Heroic Olympian's Astonishing Story of Survival as a Japanese POW in World War II* (New York: HarperCollins, 2003), 106.

Chapter 9 Discouraged

1. M. H. Manser, *Dictionary of Bible Themes: The Accessible and Comprehensive Tool for Topical Studies* (London: Martin Manser, 2009).

2. Margaret Wehrenberg, "When is Depression Not Depression? Part 2," *Psychology Today*, November 23, 2015, https://www.psychologytoday.com/us/blog/depression-management-techniques/201511/when-is-depression-not-depression-part-2.

Chapter 11 Fearful

1. A. W. Tozer, *The Pursuit of God* (Camp Hill, PA: Christian Publications, 1993), 1.

2. Andy Stanley, "Opting Out," in *Ask It: The Question That Will Revolutionize How You Make Decisions* (Colorado Springs: Multnomah, 2014).

3. Timothy Keller (@timkellernyc), Twitter post, September 12, 2014, 12:00 p.m., https://twitter.com/timkellernyc/status/510458013606739968.

4. JoHannah Reardon, "What Does It Mean to Fear God?" *Christianity Today*, February 19, 2013, https://www.christianitytoday.com/biblestudies/bible-answers/spirituallife/what-does-it-mean-to-fear-god.html.

5. William D. Eisenhower, "Fearing God," *Christianity Today*, February 7, 1986, https://www.christianitytoday.com/ct/1986/february-7/fearing-god-those-who-have-never-trembled-from-head-to-toe.html.

Chapter 12 The Power of a Thought

1. Dr. Wayne W. Dyer, "Success Secrets," *Wayne's Blog*, accessed July 18, 2020, https://www.drwaynedyer.com/blog/success-secrets/.

2. "Subconscious—Decision Making," Wonder, delivered November 5, 2019, https://askwonder.com/research/subconscious-decision-making-iz1xxf7f3.

3. Aïda Muluneh, "The Wolf You Feed," Photography and Projects, accessed August 10, 2020, https://ww.w.aidamuluneh.com/the-wolf-you-feed-1.

4. J. J. Adams, director, *Star Trek*, Paramount Pictures, 2009.

Arden Bevere is the youngest son of John and Lisa Bevere and the cofounder of Sons & Daughters, a movement committed to raising up a generation of uncompromising followers of Christ who will transform our world. Despite being just twenty-five years old, Arden has traveled the world doing ministry and speaking at conferences. He has a passion to see his generation go further than any that came before it, fully alive in this God adventure. Learn more at SonsAnd Daughters.tv, and follow Arden on Instagram or Twitter @beverearden or on Facebook.

Get to know
ARDEN

 Arden Bevere   beverearden   beverearden

Learn more about
SONS AND DAUGHTERS

www.sonsanddaughters.tv

SonsAndDaughtersTV   SonsAndDaughtersTV   SonsAndDaughtersTV

LET'S TALK ABOUT BOOKS

- Share or mention the book on your social media platforms. Use the hashtag **#Redefined**

- Write a book review on your blog or on a retailer site.

- Pick up a copy for friends, family, or anyone who you think would enjoy and be challenged by its message!

- Share this message on Twitter, Facebook, or Instagram: **I loved #Redefined by @beverearden // @RevellBooks**

- Recommend this book for your church, workplace, book club, or small group.

- Follow Revell on social media and tell us what you like.

  RevellBooks

  RevellBooks

  RevellBooks

  pinterest.com/RevellBooks